STRONGER PHOTO COMPOSITION - FOUR-STEP SYSTEM

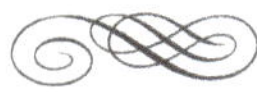

Over 100 Techniques and Tools

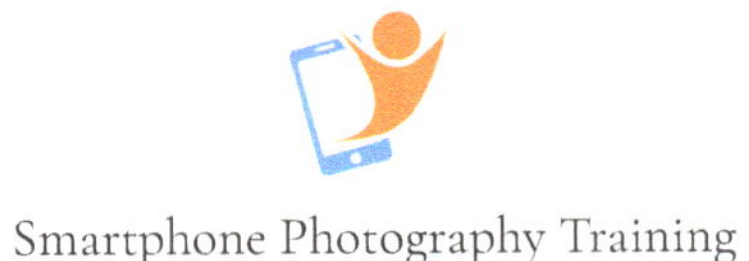

Smartphone Photography Training

STRONGER PHOTO COMPOSITION - FOUR-STEP SYSTEM

First published in 2022

Published by Smartphone Photography Training
PO Box 48 Lara, Victoria, Australia, 3212
Email: books@smartphonephotographytraining.com
URL: www.smartphonephotographytraining.com

ISBN 978-0-6456079-1-8 (Paperback)
ISBN 978-0-6456079-0-1 (eBook)

Thanks to the constant encouragement from my wife, family, friends in the mobile photography community and existing students. Without your support, this book would never have become a reality. My deepest thanks to you!

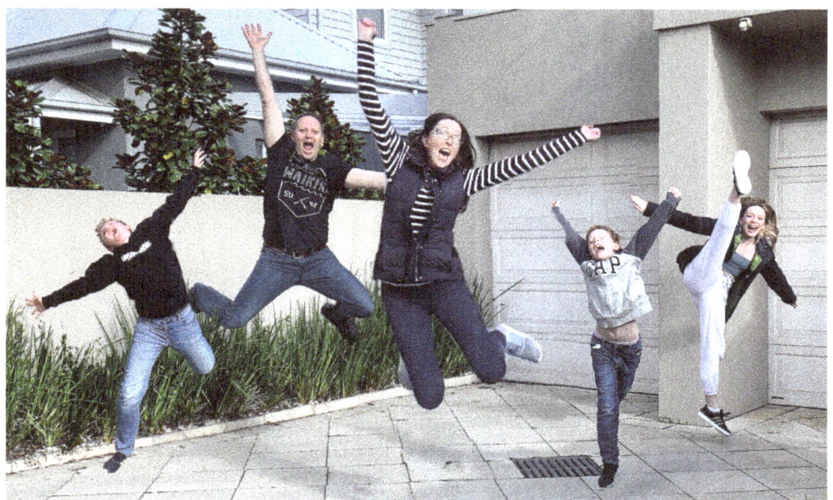

Contents

Preface 1

Principles And Elements Of Design 2

What Is Photo Composition - Why Is It Important? 6

Three Outcomes Of This System 8

Photographic Intention 10

The Story Behind This New Four-Step System 12

What Is The Stronger Composition: Four-Step System? 14

Breaking Versus Understanding The Rules 16

Visual Storytelling And Narrative In Photos 22

STEP 1 - Set Up and Position the Camera 26

STEP 2: Position the Subject in yhe Frame 60

STEP 3: Position the Contextual Elements 81

STEP 4: Enhance Composition - Mobile Editing Tools 122

Practice Activities 147

The FULL List of Composition Techniques and Tools 153

About Mike James 158

Preface

After over twenty-five years in photography, I was unsatisfied with my work. I know a lot about cameras and smartphones. So, I thought I was not creative.

Coffee with my friend and fellow professional photographer changed everything. He explained the basics of composition. It is meant to attract, hold, and guide viewers' attention through the frame to convey a photographic intent.

This epiphany sparked an obsession. I began to research all I could find about composition and design principles.

A collection of over 100 techniques and tools became overwhelming. Later, I realised I could group them into four categories — a step-by-step system. Just consider using multiple techniques from each step. You'll have a more engaging and visually expressive photo.

This book is suitable for your Android phone, iPhone, iPad, tablet, or 'big' dedicated camera. You get the point. You can apply the concepts and system to any device that takes photos!

• Mike James

Principles And Elements Of Design

Before we discuss individual elements, I want to quickly share the principles and elements of visual design with you. Since, at the end of the day, that's what photo composition truly is: the design for how we present our photos.

In my cross-industry research, I found many other design elements that traditionally have not been applied in photography. Yet, they are just as interesting when used for photography as they are in sculptures or drawings. One example is the law of enclosure (mostly used in garden design and landscaping). The law of enclosure states that creating a vertical edge that is at least 1/3 of the horizontal line creates a sense of enclosure and comfort.

This section does not form part of the Four-Step System. Rather, this is purely context to provide a bit of background information that you can utilize to design and construct photos before we get into the nitty-gritty of each tool inside our composition toolboxes.

Principles of design

Emphasis and hierarchy - Refers to which elements attract the viewer's attention and in what order. For example, imagine three people standing in a scene. The main subject, or first person, is the closest to the photographer and faces the camera, making them the largest and most prominent subject in the frame. The second person is behind the first, looking off to the side, and the third person is further away, appearing the smallest and looking away from the camera. In this example, the first subject has the most emphasis at the top of the hierarchy, and the third subject has the least emphasis at the bottom of the hierarchy. Imagine the person at the rear is the only person looking at the camera. That may change the visual hierarchy of who you notice first.

Balance and alignment - Balance in photography is the equal distribution of elements' visual weight and the attention they draw in a photo. Various factors like colour, shape, size and alignment (how things are positioned in the frame) determine the strength of emphasis on an element.

Proportion - The size of elements in the design, as they relate to each other and the design as a whole. You can use proportion to make a scene appear more natural and harmonious or make an element appear disproportionate to attract attention.

Repetition, pattern, movement and rhythm - Movement is the path the viewer's eye travels across a composition. One way this is achieved and easily observed is through the alignment of repetitive elements. The variation of size and spacing of these elements speeds up and slows down the viewer's eye, creating the pattern and rhythm in the eye movement.

Variety and contrast - Firstly, a quick definition of contrast. It is the difference between two things. High contrast is a large difference and low contrast is a little difference. Linked to emphasis and hierarchy, contrasts can occur in size, position, shape, colour, texture or orientation in a photograph. A practical example might be straight lines next to curvy lines or bright, vibrant colours next to dull, neutral colours.

Harmony and unity - Harmony and unity create a mood and sense that all elements in a photo fit together to create a single desired theme, aesthetic style, or mood. An example of this is a photo that contains a minimal analogous color range.

Space - This refers to areas in a photo without activity or subjects. You can leave space around elements to reduce clutter or vary space to create groupings, rhythm, pattern, and unity. Gosh, I could write a whole book on the effective use of space!

Elements of design

Line - These can be pre-existing in the scene, real, or implied lines between elements. Each line evokes a different response from the viewer. Vertical lines signify stability, an S-shaped curve elicits flow, and a diagonal line from the bottom right to the top left (sinister and baroque diagonal) can create visual tension.

Texture - The use of texture creates a visual focal point, contrast or balance within a design composition. Think about how the gritty sand at the beach meets the soft, smooth waves; that's an example of a naturally occurring balance of textures.

Colour - Particular colours, and even the absence thereof, have an intrinsic relationship with emotions. In addition to using dominant colours and contrasting colours, you can also try limiting your colour palette for dramatic, impactful photos.

Shape - Two-dimensional areas created through lines, implied lines, geometric, freeform or organic that are quickly recognisable, and add context for the viewer.

Form - Similar to shape, form has three dimensions: length, width and depth. You have several tools available to create depth. Layering, overlap, texture, and shadow fall-off are some visual cues that create the illusion of a three-dimensional object or scene.

Value - Measured in high to low value, white is the highest or lightest value. Conversely, black is the lowest and darkest value. Non-neutral colours also have value. Lighter colours like yellow are higher in value, and darker colours like violet are lower in value.

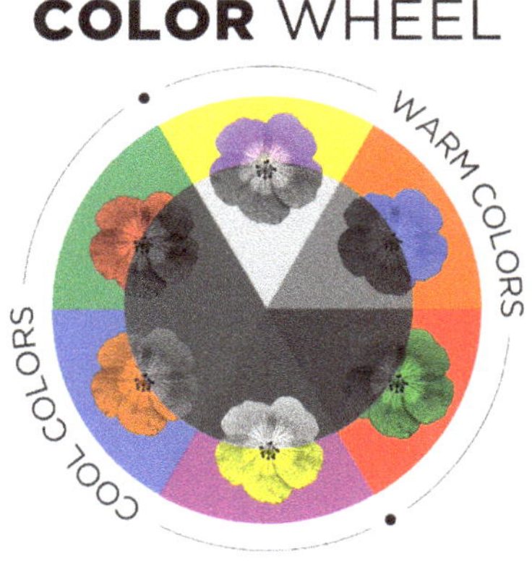

What Is Photo Composition - Why Is It Important?

In its most basic form, photo composition is how you construct a photo. Composition gives you the power to dictate points of interest in your photograph. It lets you choose elements that will capture and direct viewer focus. This creates a narrative that evokes a strong emotional response or is open to interpretation.

Our goal is to attract, hold, and guide the viewers' attention around the photo. In the same way that a painter tells a story through how they depict the 'who' and 'what' of a scene, we tell stories with visual elements in photographs. As photographers, we choose which visual elements to include or remove. We also decide how to arrange and interact with them.

Scientists studied viewers' reactions and fixation points when they looked at photos. They measured eye movements. These studies proved, time and again, that human faces, bright areas, and high-contrast areas got the most attention. By using this info to improve our photos, we can better communicate with our audience and tell more powerful stories.

Once you select and edit your visual attributes, you can create a mental hierarchy of visual points. Keeping this hierarchy in mind, you can arrange your elements and confidently create space between them. Take advantage of space in your photography by employing a systematic approach. Start with space on the X and Y axis before moving on to other techniques that create dimension and add a sense of depth.

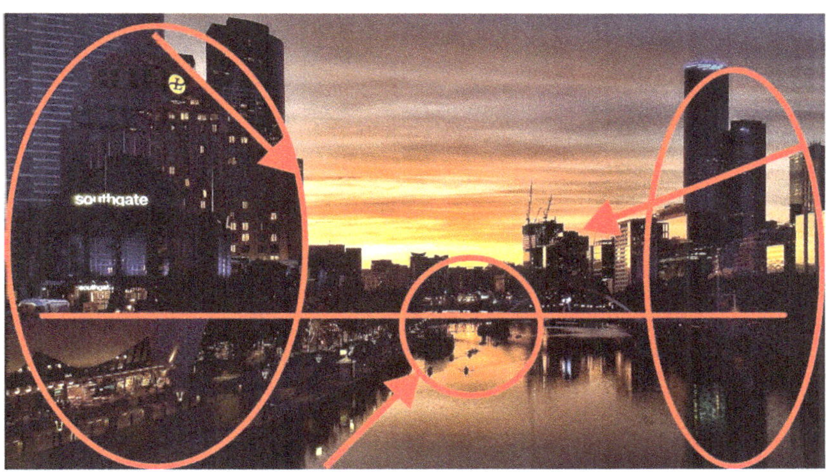

Composition is the vital blueprint that allows you to tell impactful, compelling narratives. You have a photo's story to tell. A couple's love, a busy street's shadows, or a treacherous landscape's storms. The composition is your pen

Three Outcomes Of This System

1. Intuitively select from a comprehensive list of compositional techniques and tools.

This book helps you become a more intuitive photographer. The Four-Step System will let you apply various composition techniques and tools to your photos. You won't need to think about composition or force a technique.

2. Strategic editing of photos to enhance the viewer's experience by directing their attention.

You can use photo editing tools to enhance the viewer experience. Do this as part of your photography process, no matter your subject or style. By the end of this book, you will be able to edit your photos. You will do this to attract and guide your viewers' attention to a specific spot in the image.

3. Analyze your favorite photos and identify compositional techniques and tools used.

Analyzing your favorite photos can be powerful. It helps you find what inspires and appeals to you. It also makes you more comfortable using the same techniques in your photography.

Photographic Intention

Before taking a photo, pause to recognize what motivated you to take the photo. What was the stimulus that you were reacting to? Is it the tones, colors, shapes, forms, or lighting that caught your attention?

A clear subject or story lets you experiment with different compositions. You can then find which techniques and tools support your goal.

What is photographic intention?

The intention is both the motivation and reason for taking the photo and the desired result. To improve your smartphone photos, be more intentional. This is the first step to creating meaningful images, not snapshots. Shooting with intent means you think about many aspects of your photo, including the desired outcome.

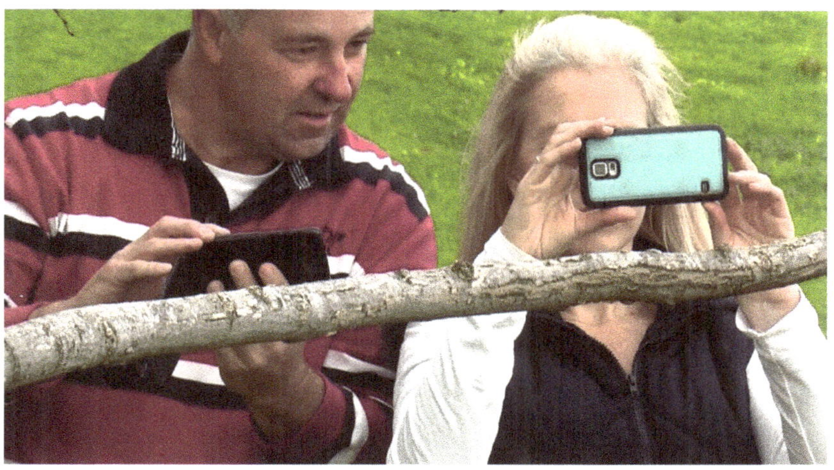

Photographic intention Vs goals

Have you noticed travellers taking photos of everything? Quite often, their photo intention is to record what is in front of them. Your intention is much more meaningful than that! When you create photos, your intent aligns with your goal in photography.

We all have different goals in photography. You may want to create a photo for social media. You want others to enjoy it. Or you want to win a photography award. You want to hang a print on your wall. If you want to win a camera club competition, research how the judge assesses the photos. This guides your choices and preparation to be more intentional in your photo capture and editing.

The Story Behind This New Four-Step System

I've worked in photography for over twenty-five years. So, I have a strong technical understanding of it. Despite this, there came a time in my career when I began to feel that my photos looked like simple snapshots. No matter what I did, my photos were flat and dull. They were dull, especially compared to the engaging photos on social media that inspired me.

Then, one fateful morning, I was having coffee with my friend, Kyle from 20West Photography. He's a fellow professional photographer. That's when everything changed. After a quiet morning of taking photos on the beach, we talked. It changed my view on creativity and photography forever.

The thing is, Kyle and I would often shoot in the same locations. Yet, my photos were coming out bland, with no depth or story. There was nothing wrong with them from a technical perspective, but they lacked vibrancy and that wow factor. They lacked the punch and pizzazz that I so admired in Kyle's and other photographers' photos.

I confessed my feelings about my work. In response, Kyle shared his creative journey in photography. He explained how he mastered many photographic rules. Then, he gave me the best photography advice I've ever received...

Instead of using learned rules, Kyle decided based on what attracted, held, and guided his attention. Instead of viewing his photos from a photographer's perspective, he was also looking at them as a viewer!

I realized that, as photographers, it's up to us to provide visual cues that engage the viewer. It's our job to use form, shape, line, color, tone, texture, and elements in a way that allows the viewer to interpret the photo in a unique way.

This epiphany sparked an obsession that would later become my passion. I researched all the compositional techniques in every art form I could think of. This included photography, painting, architecture, and garden design.

The end result was feeling paralyzed and overwhelmed when preparing a photo. My list of composition methods grew to more than 100 different techniques. I couldn't decide which techniques to use or when I should apply them. As a result, I ended up falling into the trap of repetition. I reverted to only using several basic, practiced composition techniques that I was initially familiar with. In short, I felt like I was right back to where I started.

It was a hard lesson. Yet, I learned that my repeated use of composition techniques was now hurting, not helping, my photography. Don't get me wrong, practice is, without a doubt, a necessity. And repetition can absolutely be the key to mastering a particular technique. However, overusing the same techniques stunts your growth as a photographer.

What Is The Stronger Composition: Four-Step System?

So, I had to make a change. I began creating a compositional technique glossary to keep track of what I was learning and ensure I would use it. I wrote down each technique I learned, with brief explanations. This was to add more compositional techniques to my photography.

A pattern emerged. Looking at my glossary, there were similarities between techniques. I noticed that I could list each technique under four different groups (or steps) and use those to guide my creative process. Finally, things started to click into place.

I separated these groups of techniques according to the timeline of when I could apply them while taking a photo. As I took photos, I started including at least one technique from each group/step of compositional techniques. The mix of techniques allowed me to begin with intuition. I could now create more expressive compositions with less effort.

I am eager to share all that I've learned with you, and I hope to save you some time and effort in the process.

My 'Photo Composition Stacking: Four-Step System' outlines a four-stage process for composition.

1. Set up and position the camera.

2. Position the subject in the frame.

3. Position the contextual elements.

4. Use photo editing tools to enhance the composition.

Think of each of these steps as a toolbox. Within each of these, you will have many tools at your disposal to choose from. Your choice of tools and techniques will depend on your intent. It should create a visual flow and express a narrative.

Breaking Versus Understanding The Rules

It's here that I differ from my contemporaries. I prefer to promote creativity through exploration and experimentation. It is better than teaching that the only way to be creative is to break the rules. I don't mean to say the rules can't be broken. They can. I want to show that there are many ways for photographers' creativity to flourish.

Often, deviations from classic photography techniques contradict lesser-known methods. For example, you may reframe a subject from the centred position to an off-centre position. As you can see, this deviation is an application of another technique.

Another example is the ruthless crop. It is a crop that does not seem to be applied with any compositional reasoning. This can create visual tension. It aligns with the photo's aim to be unbalanced. This may cause unease and a reaction in the viewer.

Why is composition important in mobile photos?

For a moment, think about the way the average person uses their smartphone to take photos. Often, someone will hold the camera at eye level and take the photo without much thought. This is the quickest, most common way to take snapshots. But it results in photos that lack a clear subject, mood, or creativity. This is due to the absence of intentional composition.

One of the fastest ways to improve your smartphone photography is to use its camera gridlines. They are composition guidelines.

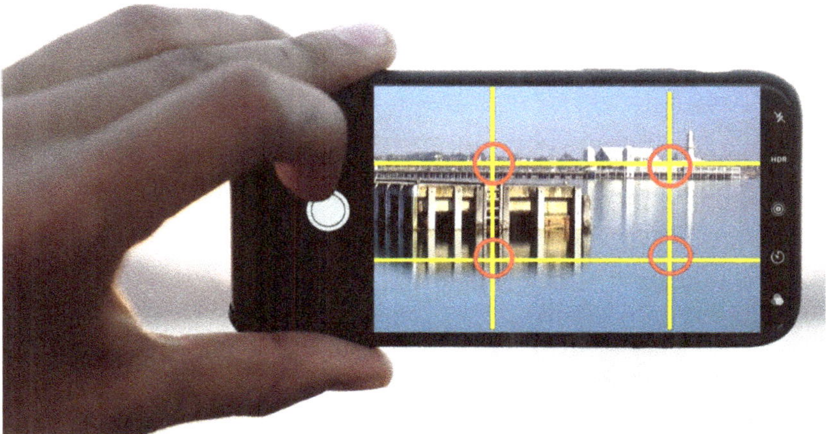

Use compositional techniques to quickly improve your photos. They will look more professional. Some amateur photographers upgrade to "dedicated" cameras. But, many pros prefer the convenience of using smartphones for personal photography.

With today's technology, you can create stunning photos. No one would believe you used a smartphone to capture them if you had the know-how.

The truth is, you can be creative and enjoy photography no matter what type of camera or device you use. All you need is an understanding of composition so thorough that it becomes intuitive.

Why learn photo composition using a smartphone?

Standalone cameras (DSLRs, mirrorless) have a range of inter-changeable lenses to choose from... *when* you have them with you. Unfortunately, not all of us can afford tens of thousands of dollars worth of camera equipment, never mind the logistics of carrying it all the time. Modern smartphones, on the other hand, have multiple lenses, and camera modes to choose from at any time.

Most amateur photographers starting out, tend to fall victim to the same temptation: constantly jumping around between options and settings to capture a range of photos. Naturally, it makes sense, as experimenting with different camera setting preferences is a great way to explore your creativity. And, it's just good old-fashioned fun. But as you go through the different practice activities at the end of this book, I encourage you to stick with the wide-angle lens, the default lens on most smartphones. I recommend exploring other lens options only once you feel confident in capturing a vast range of compositions using the wide-angle lens.

Apart from being the best quality lens in most cases, using the same wide-angle lens offers a consistent and predictable field of view. This field of view allows you to include more contextual elements while providing more distractions in the frame for you to consider using or removing. By restricting yourself from using a blurred background mode (portrait, live focus modes), you're forcing your-self to consider what's in the background.

A telephoto lens, by contrast, can crop out distracting elements in the scene. In tandem with placing the smartphone close to the sub-ject, a distant background can dramatically blur the background. We will go over different techniques involving depth of field and how you can adjust the amount of blur, more in-depth later.

Another benefit of the telephoto lens (2x or 3x lens) is the increased size of background elements. It is here that exploring new lenses can help you become more creative.

A Brief History Of Composition

Photography as an art form was invented in the 1830s, becoming more accessible. Composition and visual design have been around a lot longer.

Composition plays a vital role as an element of design in virtually every art form, regardless of the era or location. Since the earliest civilizations, wall paintings and small sculptures began as practical works. They had no perspective or defined form.

Artists have created art for thousands of years, using it for practical and entertainment purposes. Art first saw deliberate design and coherence of elements in the late 13th century. Shading, figure groupings, and perspective lines created perspective and depth.

From the Middle Ages, through the Renaissance, to modern times, composition and design have been vital to all art. This includes paintings and sculptures. Photography is no exception.

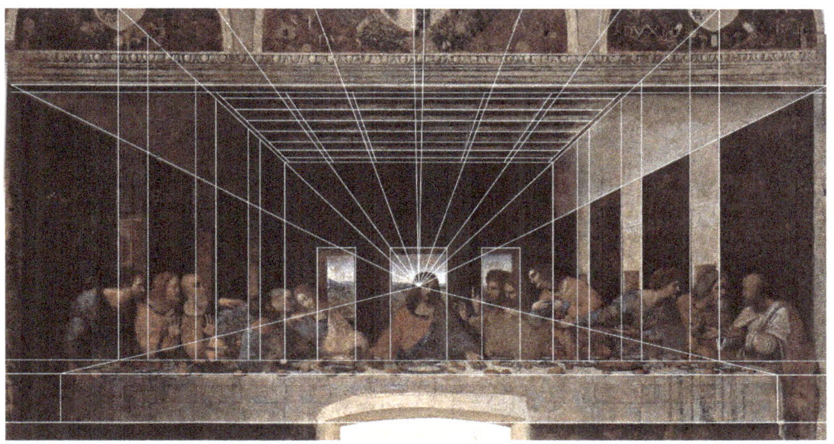

"The Last Supper" by Leonardo Da Vinci in 1489

Composition and design are notable in almost every aspect of our lives now. The concepts apply to garden and interior design, architecture, and software user experience (UX). They also apply to films and photography.

Visual Storytelling And Narrative In Photos

Storytelling is something you likely hear photographers talk about. I did not understand what that meant. Starting my photographic journey as a Private Investigator, the photos I created had to adhere to certain parameters! There was no room for creativity. A beautiful silhouette photo or intentional motion blur was useless as evidentiary photos!

What is storytelling in photography?

An example we are all familiar with is the selfie photo at a destination where you want to share where you are. The intention is to communicate where you are. Instinctively, you will likely position yourself off to the side of the frame to include the background. This is a compositional technique referred to as off-centre or the rule of thirds. The story is what context you include in the frame and how you make it clear to the viewer to interpret your story.

Storytelling is in every photography genre

One of my favourite smartphone photography genres is long-exposure landscapes. I was often wondering how you tell a story when it is just scenery. You too, may think this storytelling concept does not apply to you either.... but it does, in every photo.

My other favourite genre is macro. A close-up of an insect or inside a flower is simply capturing them. When you start combining colors, lines, and texture and chase that moment of interaction or gestures, your photos go to a whole new level.

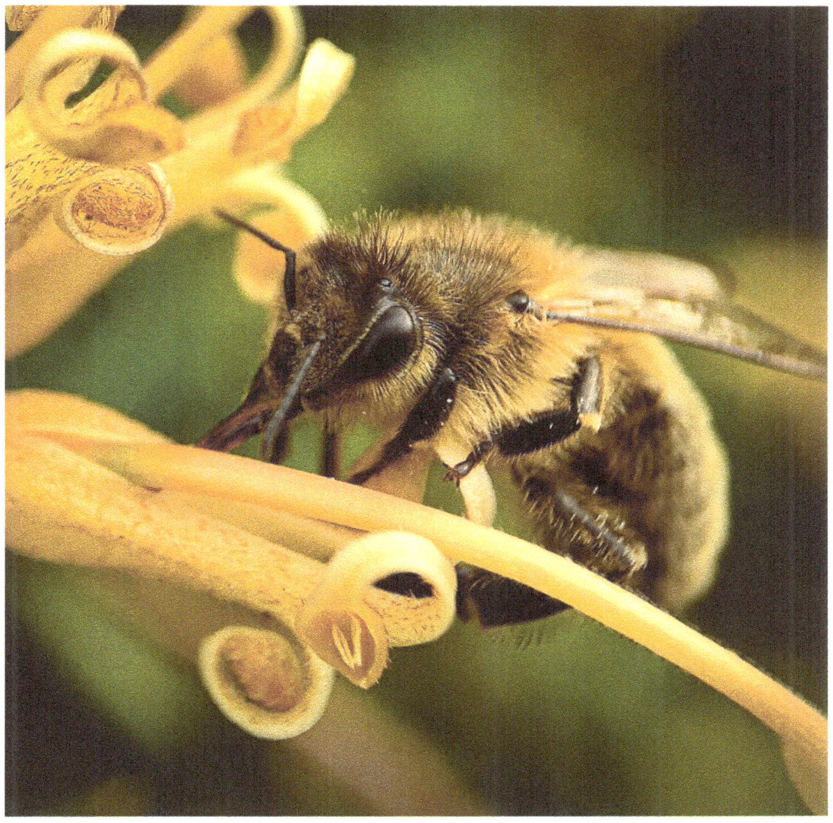

As an enthusiastic smartphone photographer, you can create insinuated stories. These are photos that provide glimpses and visual cues that are open to interpretation by the viewer. A compelling photo will engage the viewer. They will use their own experiences, culture, and biases to complete the story. The missing pieces can create a sense of mystery, tension, or drama in the photo.

Narrative

Unlike video, photography is a still moment in time that needs to encapsulate the narrative. Like writing, this can include characters, settings, subplots, drama, and tension. Storytelling does not need to be dramatic or have layers of complexity or contextual subjects in the scene. The viewer can simply be prompted to ask themselves what is happening in this photo.

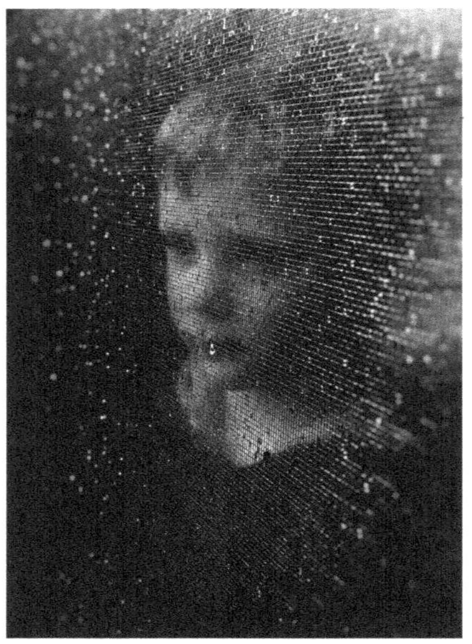

All storytelling has one constant: the moment a storyteller captures a story. Imagine the paused moment (photo) of a person walking along a waterfront. The viewer is prompted to fill in the gaps of who they are, where they have been, or where they are going. What are they wearing? What is the weather like? Ominous clouds or bright blue skies create a mood and add to the story.

In short, the narrative is the viewer's open question. It asks them to use their own experiences and imagination to answer.

STEP 1 - Set Up and Position the Camera

The first step in this 4-Step System is how to position yourself and your camera. The most dramatic improvement you can make in a composition is positioning yourself and your camera in relation to your subject. This first step is the foundation to set you up for improved results in the rest of the system.

A quick example of this is pivoting. The subject and background are fixed. You can change your position to isolate the subject against a different background. You can also walk closer to minimize digital zoom or cropping to save those valuable photo pixels!

Here are a couple of ways to reposition your camera for quick reference:

- **Roll** - tilting the whole camera horizontally, lifting the left or right edge.
- **Pitch** - tilting the top of the camera and pivoting from the bottom horizontal edge.
- **Yaw** - rotate the camera left and right along the vertical axis.
- **Height** - lift or lower the camera.

- **Distance** - step in closer or further away from the subject (minimize digital zoom and cropping).

Aside from studio shoots, we're often limited in our ability to position the subject and other elements in the scene. As no one can move mountains in a landscape, we may not always be able to move or walk around our subjects.

Yet, you can adjust the height of your camera to change the position of the horizon and other elements in the frame. You can take a few steps to the left or right to include a foreground element or create depth with a different angle.

Try changing the field of view. Use lens attachments or tilt the smartphone camera. This will create vastly different perspectives.

You can also change your location or position to accentuate existing lines, patterns, and textures further. For example, you can add energy and change the main element in the scene by rotating the smartphone and tilting the photo. A horizontal line becomes a more dynamic diagonal line. Sometimes, even minor changes can have a big impact. For example, taking a few steps to the side, finding a higher spot, or lying on the ground.

Below are some techniques to position you and the camera, and explanations of how they impact your photo composition.

Camera height and angle - change the dominance of the subject

A certain angle for the photograph creates a unique perspective, unlike typical eye-level shots. A distant, downward-facing bird's-eye view photo will make your subject look tiny against a vast background. This can be further emphasized using a wide-angle lens attachment.

.

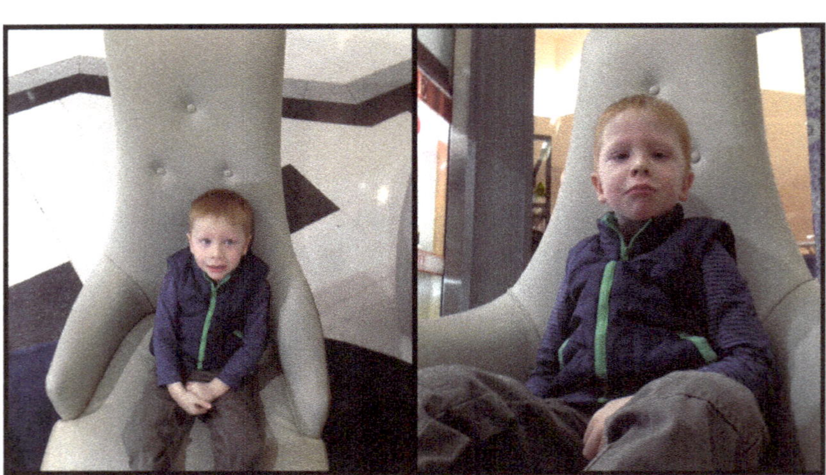

High-angled shots can make a person seem timid. Low-angle shots can make them seem more dominant. My son engaged in this example with those expressive facial gestures!

Capture angles can be applied to any genre or subject, even food. Imagine a hamburger stacked several patties tall, captured at table level compared to a photo of the same burger captured at eye level. Taking the photo at table level, or below the center of the hamburger, will improve how you communicate the burger's height. It will also let you showcase the delicious fillings spilling out of the sides. Food captures can also be at 30- or 45-degree angles for more interesting perspectives!

Camera height - intersecting background elements

The height at which you hold the smartphone camera can also

impact the background behind your subject. If you are photographing someone at the beach, for example, try different heights. See how isolating the subject's head above or below the horizon changes the photo's context and intent.

Watch out for where the horizon intersects. Doesn't the horizon in the middle of the head look like a snapshot?

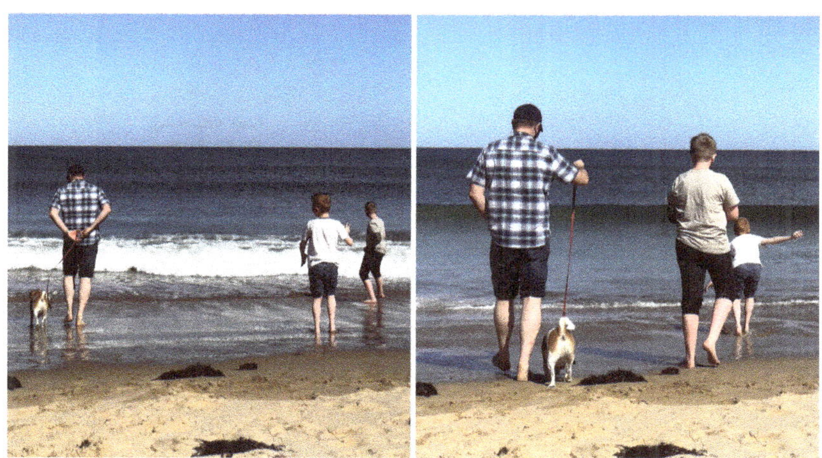

Camera height - squeeze/expand foreground

Next, we will explore the Rule of Thirds in depth. But, we'll use it briefly to position the horizon off-center for this technique. This places more emphasis on either the foreground or the sky, allowing it to take up more space in the frame. The amount of vertical space it fills is determined by the height of your camera and your physical distance to the foreground element.

Let's look at the comparison on the next page. This is a beautiful rock formation in Rye, Victoria, Australia. At sea level, the water fills about 1/6 of the frame. Or, by capturing the same scene from farther away and at an elevated height, you can see that the water fills well over half of the frame. This allows for the inclusion of the waves, whitewash, and more contextual elements in the frame.

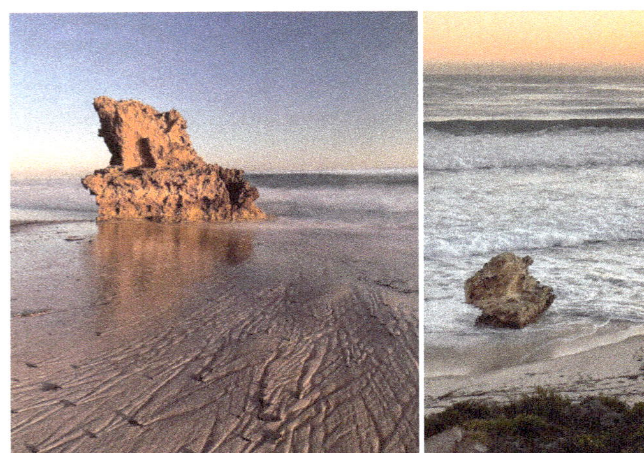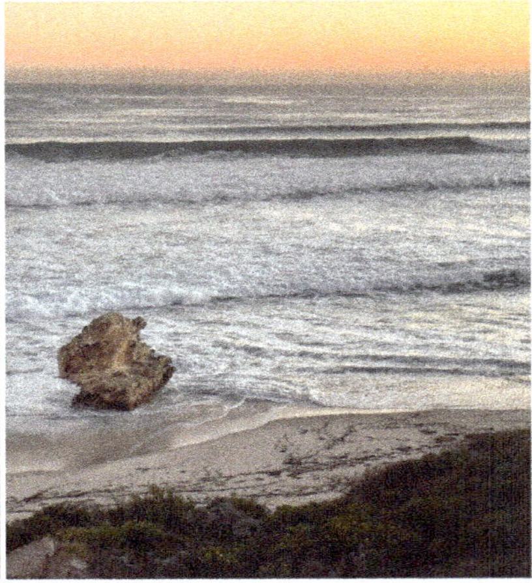

Subject to lens distortion

Objects in a photo can appear larger or smaller than they are, depending on how close they are to the camera lens. For instance, look at the street art captured at various positions. The camera position can distort the same part of the art and completely change its perspective. The main lens on a smartphone is a wide-angle lens. To reduce perspective distortion, use a 2x, 3x, 5x, or telephoto lens on the dedicated camera. Then, step back from a front and centred position.

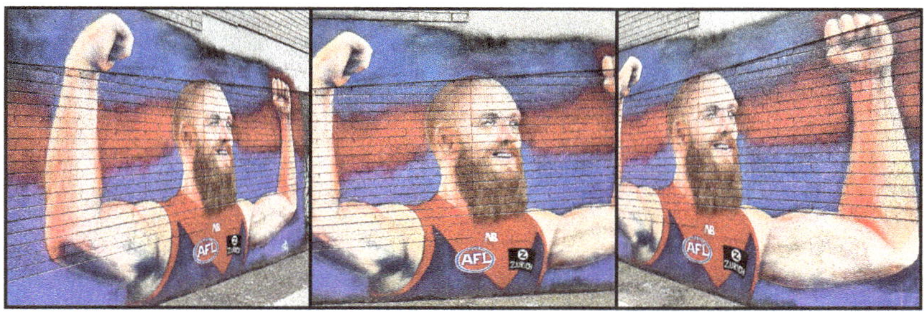

Different lenses, like super-wide, wide-angle, and telephoto, can alter your subject's size. They can make it appear smaller or larger than it is. This is especially true with different focal length lens attachments. They can create depth and add a creative flair to your photos.

Lens compression - flattening the photo?

Lens compression causes background elements to appear bigger and closer to the foreground than they are in reality. Looking at the photos below, notice how the sheds in the background of photo 4 look much farther away than in photos 2 and 3. That's because we perceive distant objects as being smaller. As discussed before in 'Subject to lens distortion,' objects closer to the lens look larger.

Many photographers think they need an expensive telephoto lens to flatten the photo and bring the background closer. But you can achieve the same effect as a smartphone photographer thanks to zoom lens attachments. Some smartphone models now have exceptional optical zoom. Others still have a long way to go!

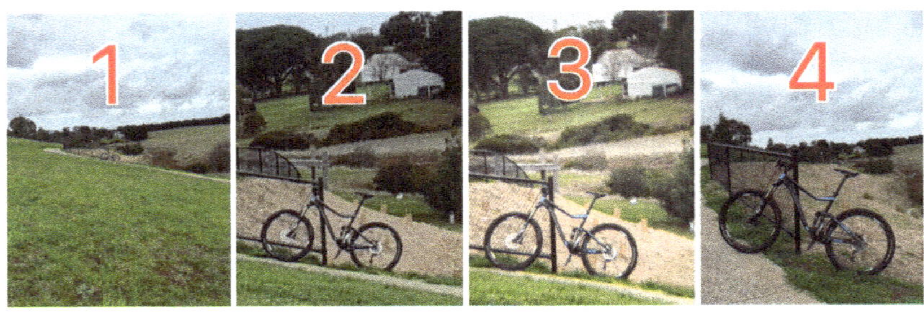

Let's take another look at each of the photos above and examine how I took each photo.

1. Default wide-angle iPhone camera captured at approximately 30 m away. I cropped photo one to the same zoom level as photo three.

2. iPhone capture with a 14x lens attachment from the same position at 30 m away.

3. This image is the default wide-angle lens, zoomed in. Notice the improved image quality in image 2?

4. Default wide-angle iPhone camera was captured at approximately five meters away.

Let's use these photos to debunk one of the most common theories about photo compression. Photo compression has nothing to do with lens choice. As you can see, photo two (photo one, cropped) is almost identical to photo three. It is difficult to observe in a printed book. However, the 14x lens attachment improves the resolution in the center of the frame in photo three. There is also no distortion or compression difference compared to photo two. And when you move closer to the subject (photo four), the composition of the background is very different.

If you stand farther back with a zoom lens, the background will appear larger. It will provide more context for your viewer.

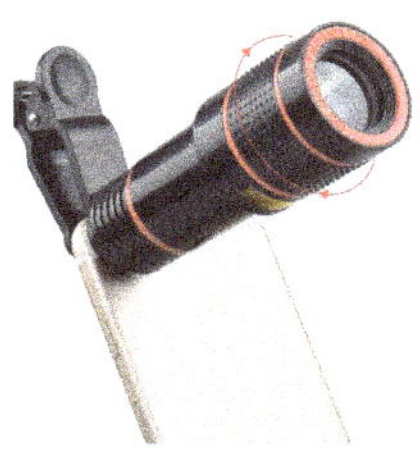

Note: Any 14x telephoto lens attachment has degraded quality. The unavoidable physics involved causes fringing (coloured edges) and other optical issues. Photo editing can easily minimize these issues. So, I still recommend lens attachments. They can expand your smartphone's capabilities and add flexibility to your photo options.

Perspective – lens distortion

Rectilinear lenses (fixed, zoom, wide-angle) make lines straight in photos. Curvilinear lenses (fisheye) bend straight lines in photos with a striking effect. Let's discuss other lens types and their distortions. You can use them as compositional tools in your photography.

Barrel distortion causes straight lines in the photo (like walls, stairs, etc.) to bend outward from the center. This is common in wide-angle lenses. They try to force a wider view onto a photosensor that can only handle a smaller one.

Pincushion distortion causes straight lines in the photo to bend inward from the frame's edges. This occurs in zoom lens attachments. The camera captures a smaller field of view than the photo sensor.

So, the system needs to stretch it to fit the frame. Smartphone photos with a long zoom lens look best when cropped to remove the blurred edges and distortion.

You may be asking, "Why is Mike mentioning these in the position section of the compositional book?" Well, that's because you can further exaggerate the effect of these distortions with your camera or smartphone placement.

As an example, check out the photo below. Notice how the combination of a fisheye lens and a low-positioned camera provides a unique perspective.

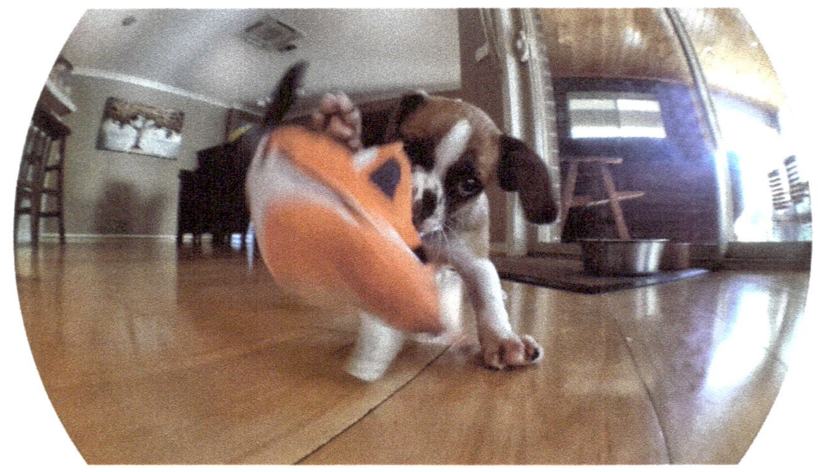

Tilt distortion

This is one of those shooting techniques that you need to be aware of to create an accurate representation of a scene. You can easily exaggerate the distortion for a creative effect. Like most compositional tools, it can be emphasized in editing.

Did you know that real estate photographers always set their tripods to the precise midpoint of the floor and ceiling? It's true! On average, most real estate photographers use wide-angle lenses just like the default camera in our smartphones. And, as we have covered, objects closer to the lens appear bigger and objects farther away from the lens appear smaller. So, when the camera is held below or above the midpoint at a tilt, the photo will attempt to converge at the top or bottom.

Tilt distortion is especially clear in tall buildings, like cathedrals and churches. Since it is impossible to get to the midpoint in those kinds of locations, the result is that the vertical walls appear to converge.

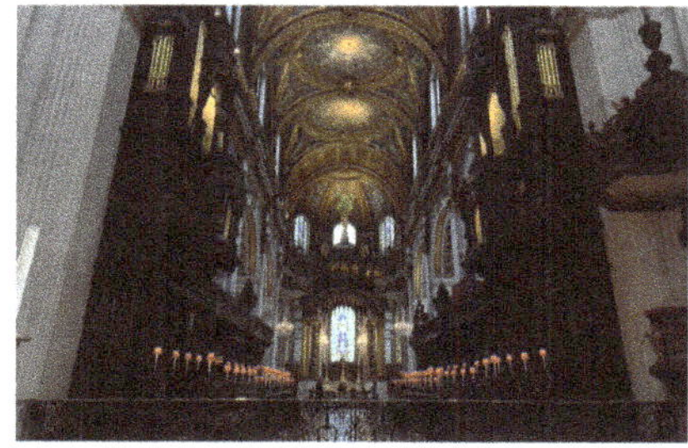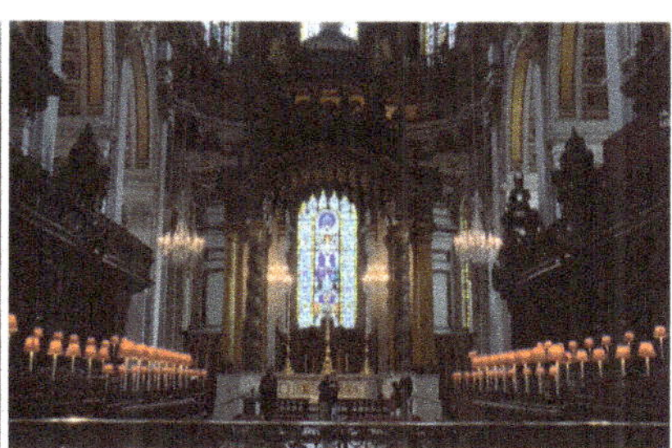

Be mindful when correcting this in editing, as you may inadvertently crop the scene a little. You can prevent this while capturing the photo by leaving space around the essential content in the scene.

Symmetry - vertical, horizontal

A symmetrical photo is easy to explain. Imagine that you could print your photo on see-through paper and fold your picture in half vertically or horizontally. If the photo is mirrored on both sides, then your photo is symmetrical.

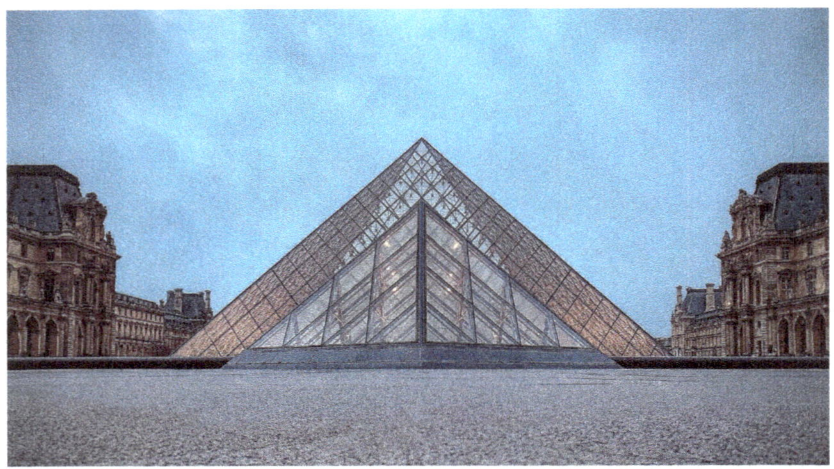

Symmetrical means that both sides of the frame have equal weight. This gives the picture-perfect balance and makes it pleasing to the eye. Seeking out vertical or horizontal symmetry in your photos is a great way to help simplify the photo.

Symmetry - spiral and radial balance

Radial balance has a central focal point. Multiple lines or elements extend in a circle around it. These multiple lines work like a magnet for viewer attention, grabbing focus and forcing it toward the central point.

These are usually clean, simple, and powerful photos, without distractions. The swirling lines of a spiral can have a calming, almost hypnotic effect. Two obvious examples are a spiral staircase and a wheel with spokes radiating away from the central hub.

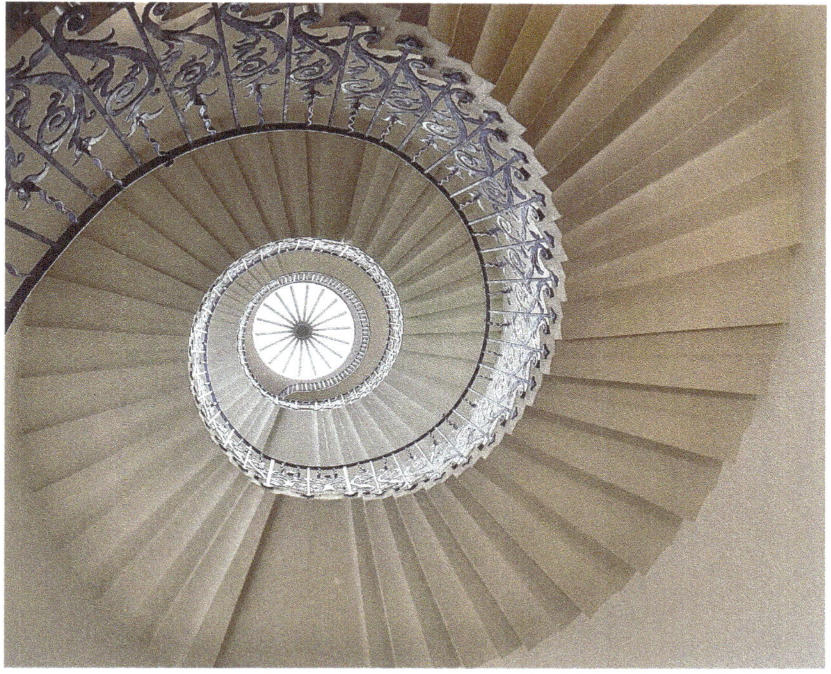

Symmetry - crystallographic or mosaic balance

Crystallographic or mosaic balance is balanced chaos! This type of composition is like patterns and repetition. But it doesn't need a distinct subject or focus to succeed. Instead, the elements are equally represented in the frame and have a more 'uniform' emphasis.

At first glance, the lack of a prominent or isolated subject leads to visual noise. You cannot discard crystallographic photos as a "happy snap," as the intention of the photo (to create balance) is evident and draws the viewer in.

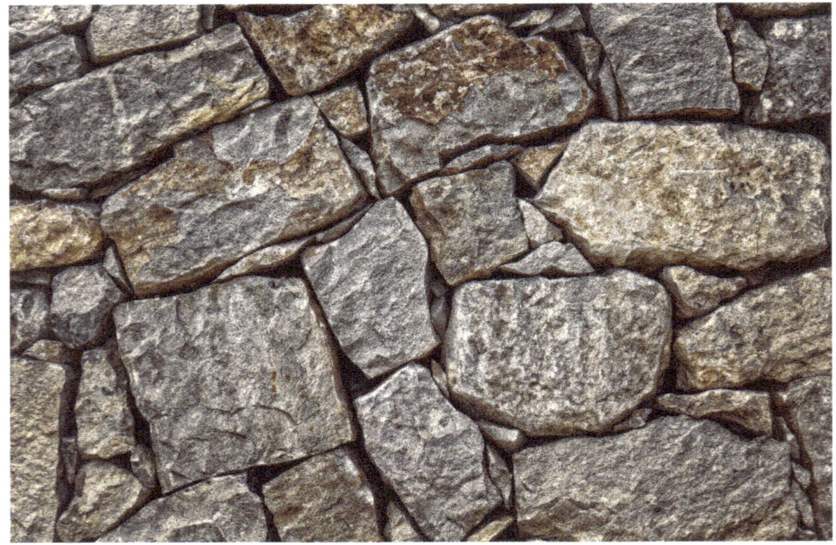

Don't forget to experiment with scale and proportion. Randomly sized elements can make the photo feel more appealing and natural. If some elements become isolated or stand out, try a monochromatic edit. Or, use complementary colors to help restore balance.

This style of photo serves as an excellent textured background in double exposure photos.

Asymmetrical balance - (aka informal balance)

An asymmetrical photo, as you may have guessed, is the opposite of a symmetrical photo. Asymmetrical photos differ when split down the center, unlike perfectly mirrored photos.

Asymmetrical balance uses elements of different sizes and positions to create balance. They are on either side of the frame. Using space lets you balance the photo. It draws the viewer's attention equally.

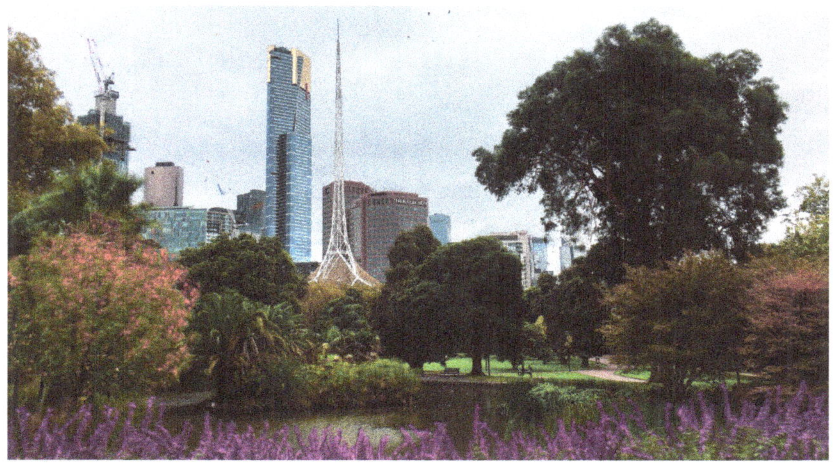

Additionally, several smaller, individual objects on one side of the frame balance a single larger object on the opposite side. Extra space on one side of a photo can also be used to create balance and even out the visual weight in a photo.

Unique perspective - look up

We all live our lives viewing the world at eye level. A deviation from that perspective can be appealing at once and grab our attention.

At a workshop in Melbourne, I demonstrated this by taking a photo. It shows a view straight up between buildings in a popular laneway.

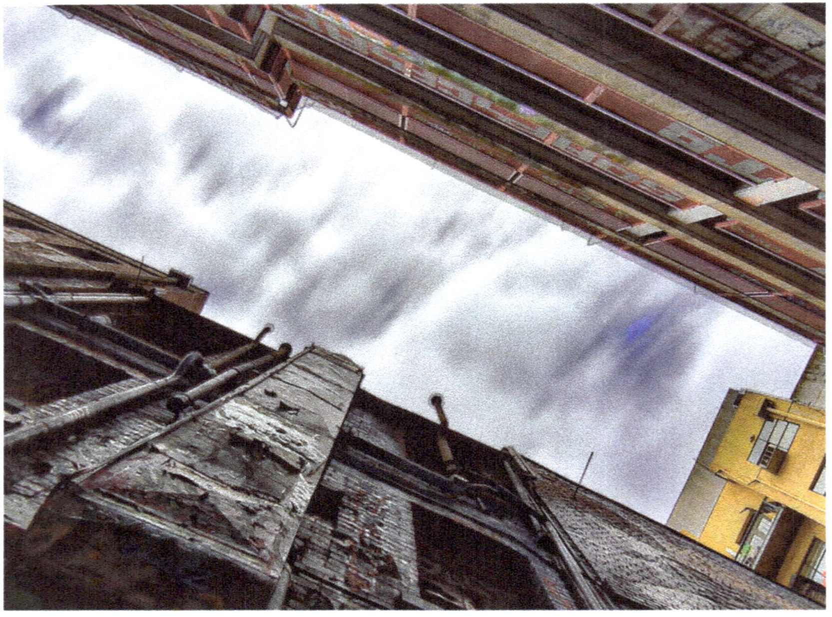

This laneway's graffiti is photographed hundreds, if not thousands, of times a day. And yet, I have never seen anyone shoot upward, capturing this unique perspective of the location.

Unique perspective - shoot at ground level

I love macro photography for many reasons. It opens new experiences and lets you see the unseen. Getting down on ground level forces you to take your time... especially if you're like me, and it takes effort to get back up!

Everything looks bigger and more significant from a low vantage point. Shooting up at your children and pets can help you find an otherwise unexplored, exciting perspective. Plus, it's fun to get down to their level and see the world as they do!

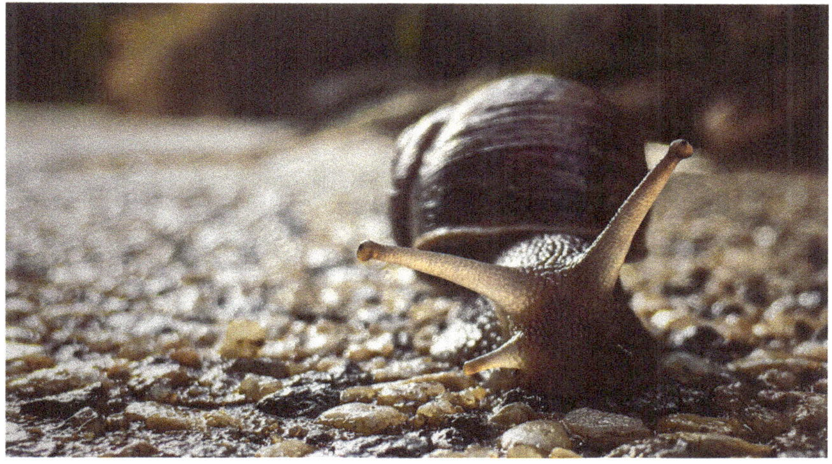

Light - direction, strength, and quality

I'm sure you've heard that photography is all about beautiful lighting. As the sun moves across our sky, we enjoy varying light strengths and directions.

By changing your position around the subject, you have some control over the light direction in your photo. For example, when the sun is low in the early morning or late afternoon, you can point your smartphone at the sun and get a high-contrast backlight. This effect, in particular, can make subjects look fantastic, with back-lights creating a halo effect around the edges.

In the opposite direction, front lighting can minimize shadows on your subject. We have all seen the overhead-lit portraits where people's foreheads cast shadows on their eyes (raccoon eyes). In this situation, you can avoid shadows by repositioning the light source.

Clouds are your friend when photographing outdoors. They serve as huge light diffusers, lifting shadows in your scene.

Some photographic genres require a delicate balance. This is especially true for product and food photographers. They must find the perfect mix of lighting direction, strength, and quality.

Landscape photographers will use apps like PhotoPills. They want to know the sun's direction at dawn and dusk. This is valuable to ensure that you compose for the light, as well as the subject, depth, and supporting elements.

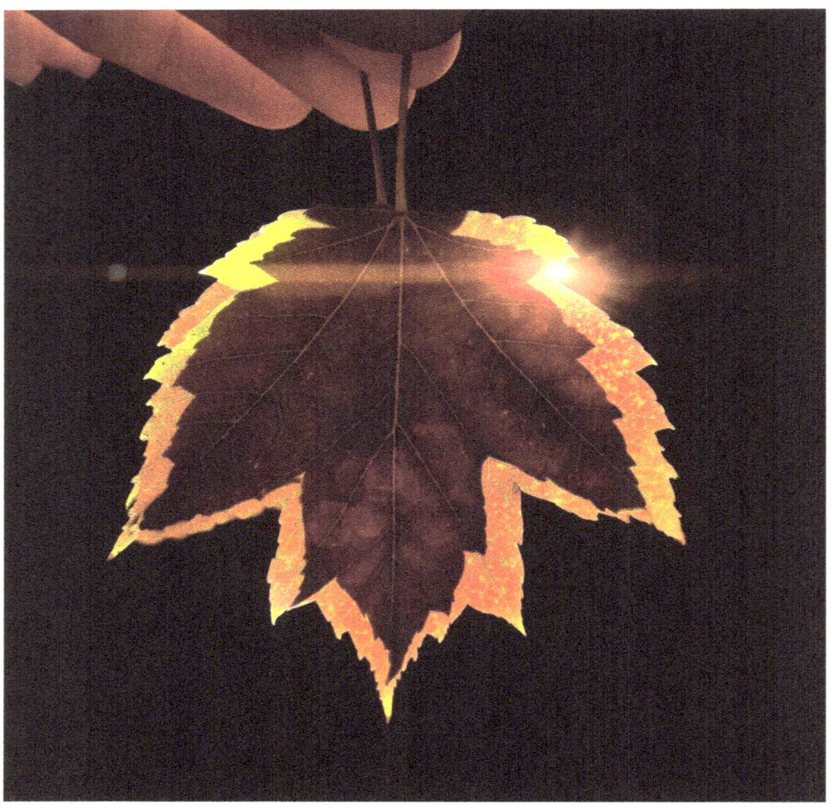

Light - hard light creates shadows

Another common misconception in photography is that the best photos are only attainable during the golden hours of the day. This is because the sun is high in the sky during the middle of the day, creating the strongest shadows.

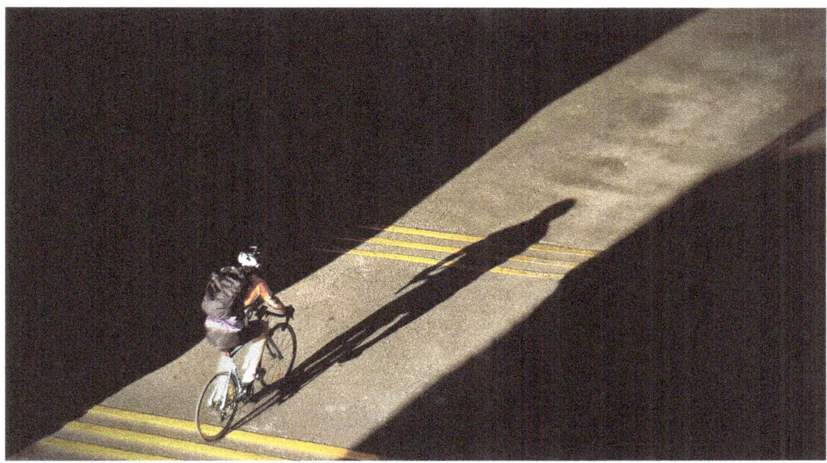

Shadows of varying strengths can assist in communicating shape and form through your photo elements. When capturing street photos, look for opportunities where harsh shadows frame a particular area. Anticipating a person entering and casting a long shadow can reward you, as in the photo above.

Light - Side lighting creates texture and depth

In photography, textures are all about the visual quality of the small surface details of an object. In your photo, you are trying to replicate what the object looks like in 3D.

Why is this in Step 1 - Position of Your Camera? That's because, by moving your smartphone camera, you can use side lighting. It will create shadows behind the taller part of the texture and reveal more detail. Take a look at how the shadows accentuate different textures in the following example.

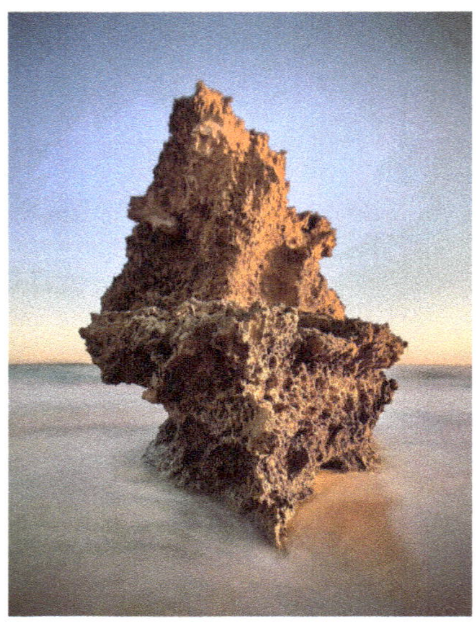

Flat lay - bird's-eye view

A flat lay is a bird's-eye view photo taken directly above objects that have been arranged and styled on a flat surface. A perfect example of composition stacking, flat lays need you to place objects to create shapes and lines. After finding a flat surface, this technique requires practice. It needs experimentation with lighting, object arrangement, layering, color, and texture.

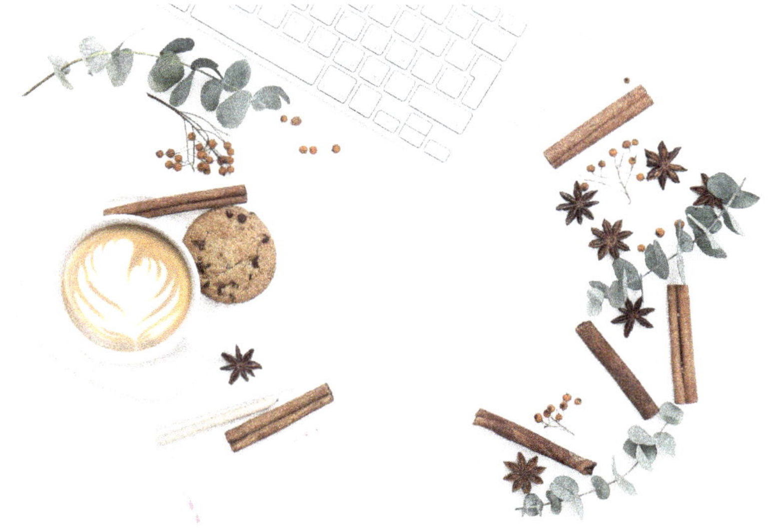

The key is to place the larger items down first, then layer smaller items into the frame to create your context. Remember, sometimes less is more and can be more impactful than cluttering the photo.

Reflections

I love shooting reflections. The options are limitless. They range from reflective surfaces on buildings to shooting across puddles. You may even see me carrying a bottle of water... just to make my own puddle! And I recommend you do the same.

Reflections are great for mirrored photos. They create symmetry where it wouldn't exist. Including a visual reference of where you have captured the reflection, like a window frame, can add extra visual interest.

You can also boost viewer engagement in reflection photos. The viewer must recognize that the photo is of a reflection, not the object. By the time the viewer has that 'aha moment' of figuring out it's a reflection, you have achieved the engagement that can be so elusive.

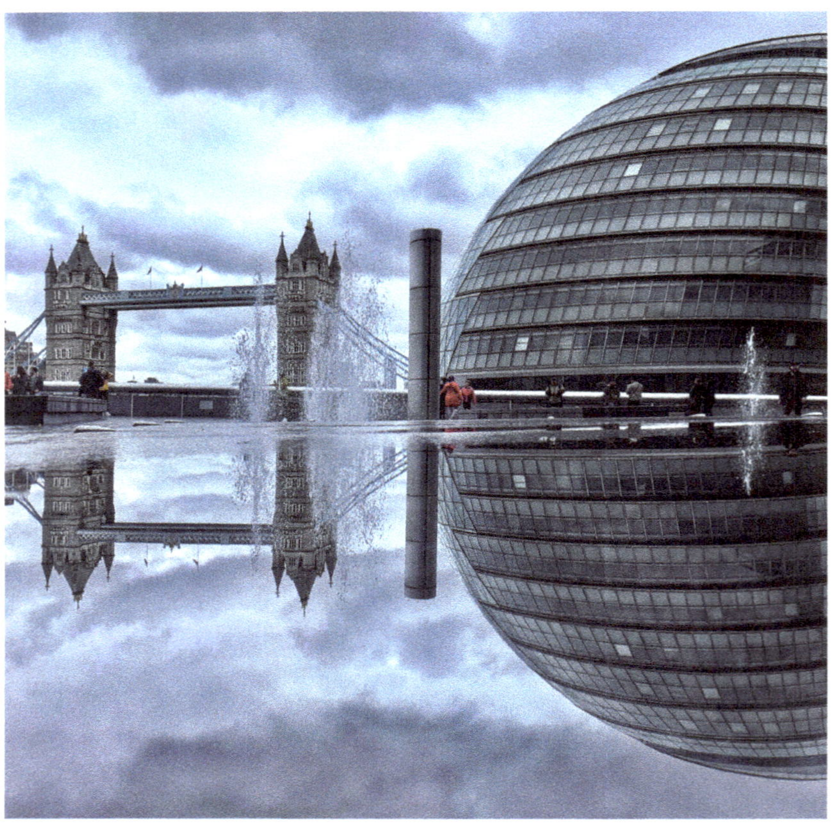

The best tip I can share for capturing a reflection in a puddle is to hold your phone upside down and position the lens close to the water. Make sure that the main subject is isolated from the background in the reflection. This could be as simple as using space between buildings or contrasting elements.

Front lighting will ensure a nice, bright reflection full of vibrant colors.

Over-the-shoulder - third-person perspective

The over-the-shoulder perspective is a powerful technique. It is also known as a third-person shot. It makes viewers feel as if they are taking the photo.

Including a person's shoulder in the foreground creates a visual anchor. It implies a line of sight to what they're looking at.

Chances are, you've already seen this technique in practice in your favorite television shows and movies. That's because the third-person perspective forces viewers into the scene, allowing us to feel as if we're in the moment with the characters. Being so close to the person's shoulder creates a sense of intimacy and lets the viewer connect with their perspective on a new level.

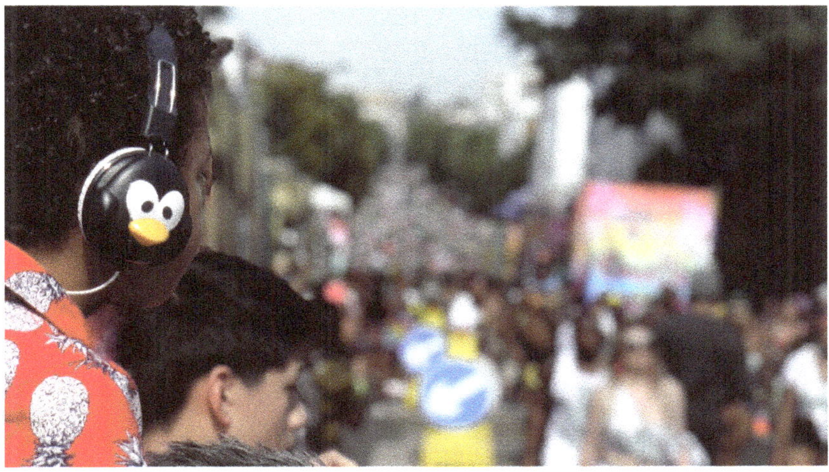

When using the over-the-shoulder technique, compare shots. See how much of the subject's shoulder to include. Pay attention to the subject's height, size, and space in the frame. Also, consider whether to tap on the subject's shoulder or background on the screen to change the focus point on your smartphone camera. By blurring either the shoulder or the background, you can create a greater sense of depth or beautiful bokeh.

As covered before, the closer you are to the subject's shoulder and the distance to the background will affect the strength of the blur. You can always add more blur in Step 4 of the system.

Keystone distortion

This technique involves getting up close to a tall object like a building or tree and tilting your smartphone upwards. You could also do it from the top of a tall feature and point down, so long as it's safe to do so! The building will look like it is leaning and appear to get broader toward the top.

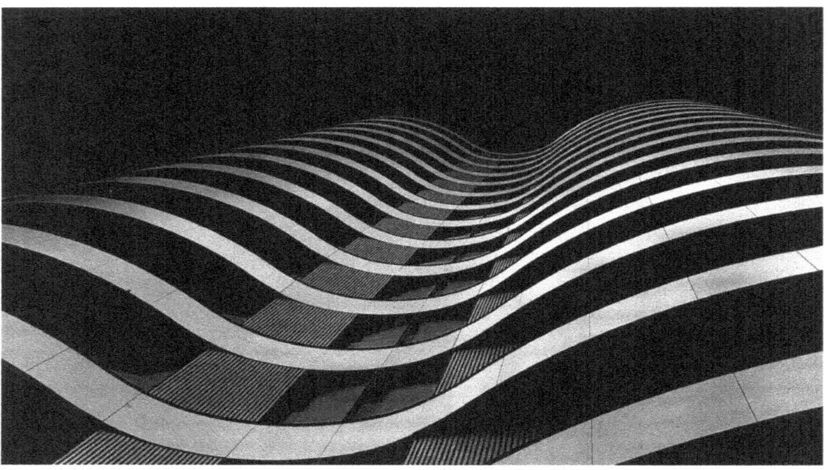

We call the process of correcting this distortion keystoning. But if you want to use or even strengthen the effect, you can use distortion-correction tools to exaggerate it.

Two-point perspective

To add even more depth to a photo, you can capture the corners of an object's sides, creating two vanishing points along the sides.

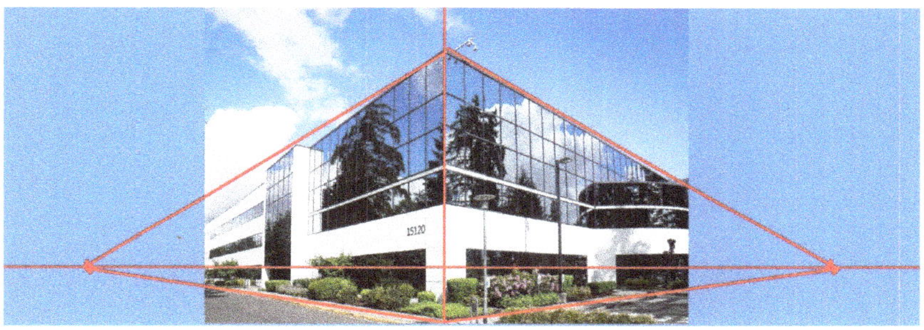

Remember, the actual converging spot does not need to appear in the photo; the goal is to have parallel lines start to converge. This technique works well for buildings with outward-stretched walls. It adds depth.

Three-point perspective

Also, in the two-point linear perspective, you can shoot from a lower or higher angle to bring in a vertical convergence. A three-point perspective is common for vehicle photography. The photographer shoots from opposite the front corner and at a lower angle. The low vertical angle can make vehicles look larger and more imposing. It's perfect for masculine vehicles.

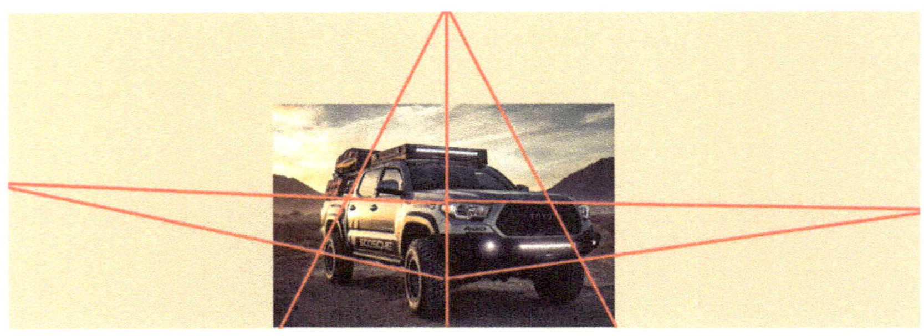

Diminishing scale perspective

Our brains perceive smaller objects to be farther away than larger, closer objects. And, as covered before in the section 'subject to lens distortion,' objects closer to the lens appear larger.

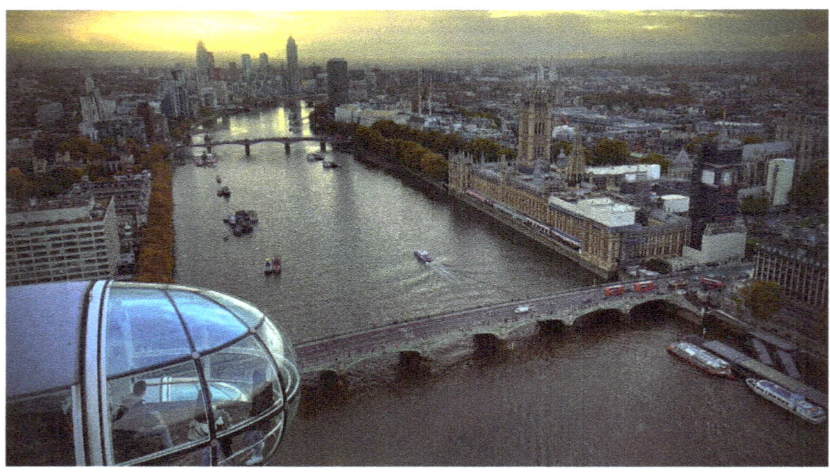

We can use this to our advantage to create a sense of depth by including (or further emphasizing) the varying sizes of elements in your composition. The shift in size from the foreground to the background makes the composition appear three-dimensional.

Atmospheric perspective

Also called aerial or atmospheric perspective, distant objects look lighter. Colors also become more muted. This occurs because we are looking through more air containing more particles when we look over distances.

To use this depth technique in your photos, try to shoot when you see particles, like fog or dust, in the air. Another way you can take advantage of atmospheric perspective is by capturing photos in the snow, as you can see in the example below!

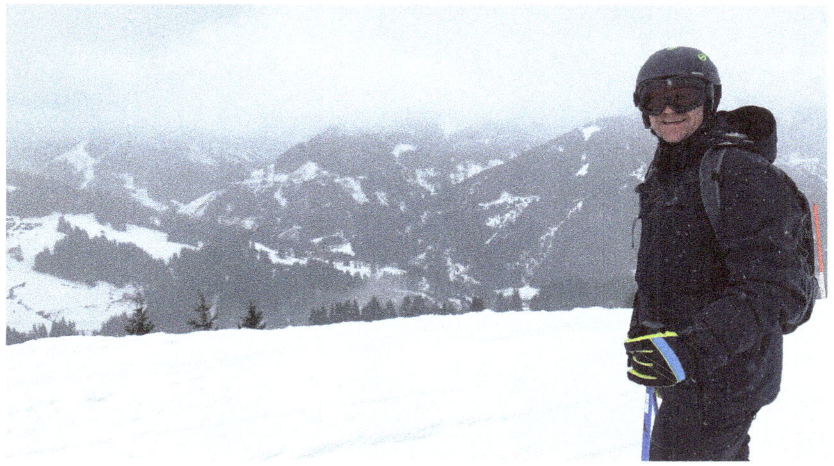

Fog photos are only interesting if at least one area is clear. The contrast creates the desired depth. Later in Step 4 of the system, you can use the editing steps in the Orton effect to create or emphasize atmospheric perspective.

Forced perspective

Have you ever tried to take a photo of a sunset with your smartphone? It was disappointing that the distant objects were tiny on the screen. If so, you've seen forced perspective or distance-to-camera distortion.

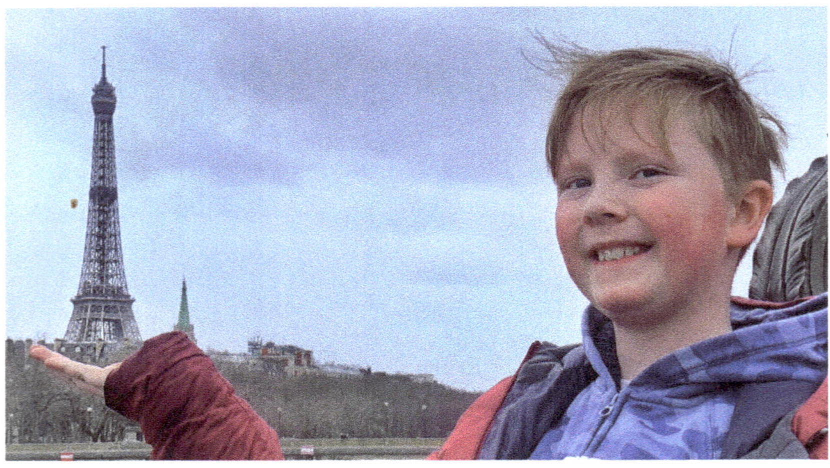

A classic example of forced perspective is in photos of people posing with distant, larger objects, like the Leaning Tower of Pisa. You can create a forced perspective by choosing a capture angle with a more distant background. This works without changing your distance from the subject.

Your smartphone gives you more freedom to create a forced perspective. Use editing apps like PicsArt (Android, iOS) and Handy-Photo (iOS). For example, you can remove and shrink background elements. Then, place them back on the original photo to further emphasize the perspective distortion. This process is also known as compositing.

Orientation and aspect ratio

I prefer to edit my photos in a 16:9 aspect ratio because I display a rotating selection of my favorite shots on my widescreen TV.

Depending on the photo's content and context, a 9:16 (portrait) aspect ratio may work better. It's ideal for Instagram stories.

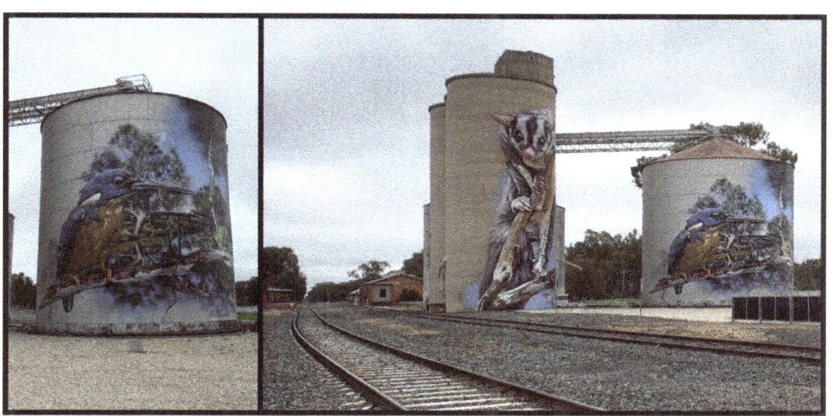

Choosing whether to capture a vertical or horizontal photo can change the whole composition of the photo. The examples above show how the composition changes when the photo's orientation changes from vertical to landscape.

Some genres and subjects naturally lend themselves to either a vertical or a horizontal capture. Most landscape scenes use horizontal (landscape) orientation. Portraits often use vertical (portrait) orientation. You can mix it up by forcing yourself to capture a landscape by holding the phone/camera in a vertical orientation and vice versa!

Corner to corner

Some compositional techniques are specific to certain genres of photography. A typical real estate photo, for instance, is taken from one corner of a room towards the opposite corner. This is because shooting corner to corner does two things. It makes the photo look more three-dimensional. It also brings more floor into the scene, creating a greater sense of space.

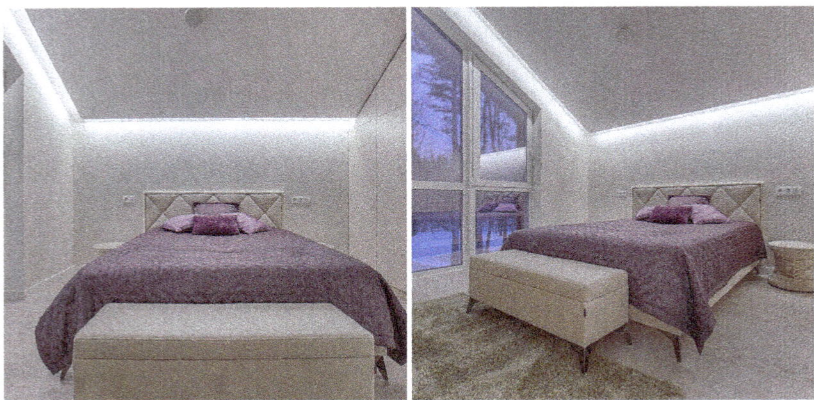

One of the main intentions of interior photography is to make the viewer feel like they are there and experience that space. Shooting corner to corner creates an angled view. It's more effective. It's like how we observe spaces in daily life. We spend more time looking around our home, through open areas than staring straight at a wall (unless there is a TV on it, of course).

Shoot toward space

I risk this becoming all about real estate photography. But, I want to share a compositional technique often used in the genre: shooting towards open space.

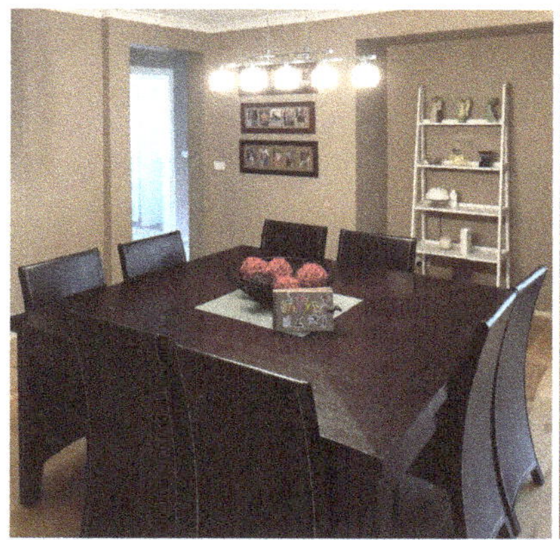 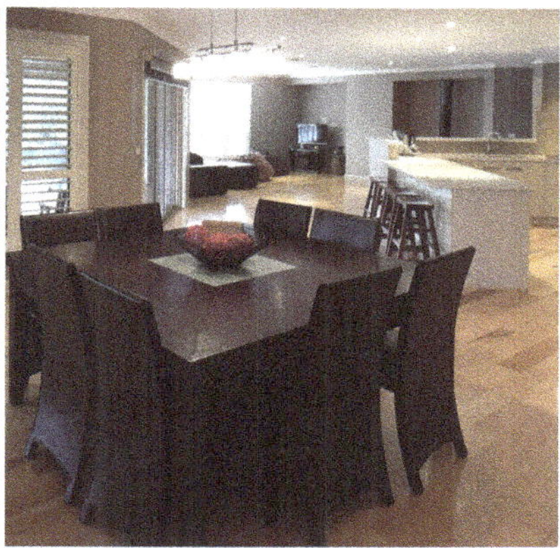

Shooting towards areas with the most space encourages the viewer to look beyond the scene immediately in front of them. Doorways and walkways leading out of the frame can spark wonder. Viewers may ask, "Where does that lead?"

Vertical panoramic

Panoramic mode on our smartphones is incredible, so much so that I have a $500 pano tripod head that has been collecting dust for years! Most smartphones feature an arrow that you can tap twice to start the pano recording and switch the recording direction.

A popular photo opportunity in Melbourne is the Melbourne State Library. The library's level 6 has a lovely view. It overlooks the dome gallery and the dome reading room below. People often take photos from that spot. Unfortunately, most fail to capture all the context. They hold their phones vertically.

The secret is to turn your smartphone horizontally and enable panoramic mode. Then, move your camera vertically.

Walking panoramic

If you take a sweeping pano photo without moving, the start and endpoints may appear further away. This will create a warped photo. The secret to avoiding this scenario is to start at one end of the scene you're photographing and tap the capture button. Then, walk steadily along the scene while keeping the same distance. Either tap the capture button at the end or move your smartphone the opposite way to stop the recording.

I know this is more of a quick capture lesson than a composition technique. But, this technique lets you consider using a panoramic mode in your compositions when taking photos.

Look at the examples below and see if you can determine which mode each photographer used to take the photos.

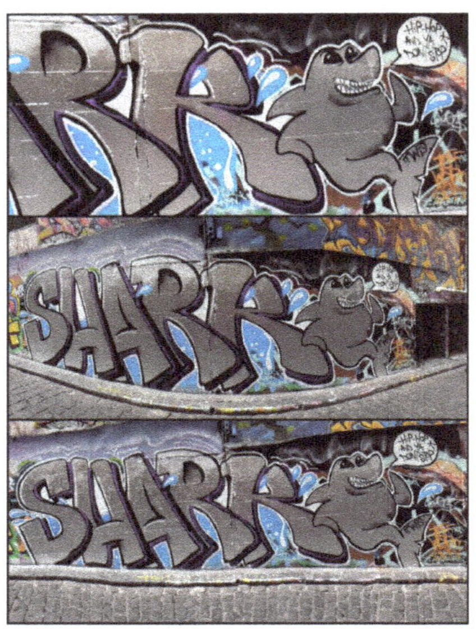

Dutch angle - rotate the smartphone

Also known as Dutch Tilt, German Angle, Canted Angle, or Oblique

Angle. This non-traditional compositional technique makes the horizon or vertical lines appear 'intentionally' angled. The easiest way to achieve this is to hold your phone at an angle as you shoot.

To achieve this, hold the phone or dedicated camera in the horizontal, landscape orientation. Next, lift either the left or right edge upwards or downwards. How much will be a matter of experimentation? Remember not to tilt the top edge of the phone back and forth.

Cinematographers use this technique for a dramatic effect. It shows movement, energy, unease, and frantic action. Street photography, in particular, benefits from this technique.

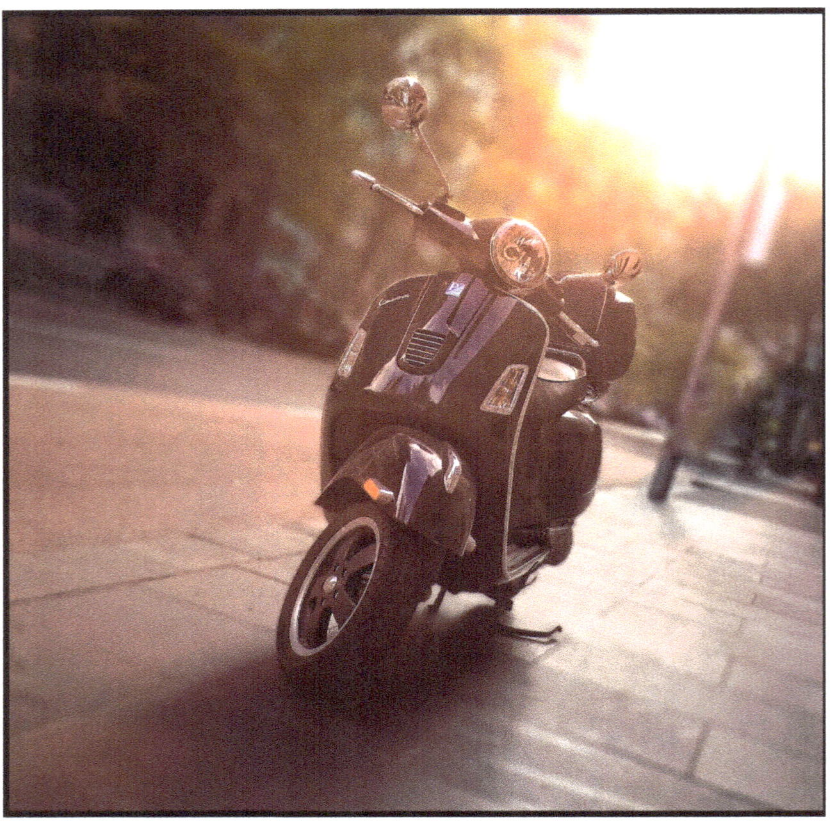

Be mindful that this technique involves more than rotating the photo. The photos in Step 2 show that your framing affects the viewer's feelings. So does the direction in which you rotate the camera.

Step 1 - list of techniques

Camera height - subject
Camera height - background
Camera height - foreground
Subject to lens distortion
Lens compression
Perspective – lens distortion
Tilt distortion
Symmetry - vertical, horizontal
Symmetry - spiral and radial
Symmetry - crystallographic
Asymmetrical balance
Unique perspective - look up
Unique perspective - ground level
Light - direction and quality
Light - hard light
Light - Side lighting

Flat lay - bird's-eye view
Reflections
Over-the-shoulder
Keystone distortion
Two-point perspective
Three-point perspective
Diminishing perspective
Atmospheric perspective
Forced perspective
Orientation and aspect ratio
Corner to corner
Shoot toward space
Vertical panoramic
Walking panoramic
Dutch angle

STEP 2: Position the Subject in yhe Frame

Now that we've covered how to position yourself and your smartphone camera in the last section, we can move on to Step 2. This is where we position the main subject... the hero of the photo.

You will notice that some of the following compositional techniques may cross over into the 4 different steps. For example, filling the frame uses the main subject to take up most of the photo, if not all of it. You could also list this technique in Step 1: Positioning the Camera, as you can consider it a way of getting in close.

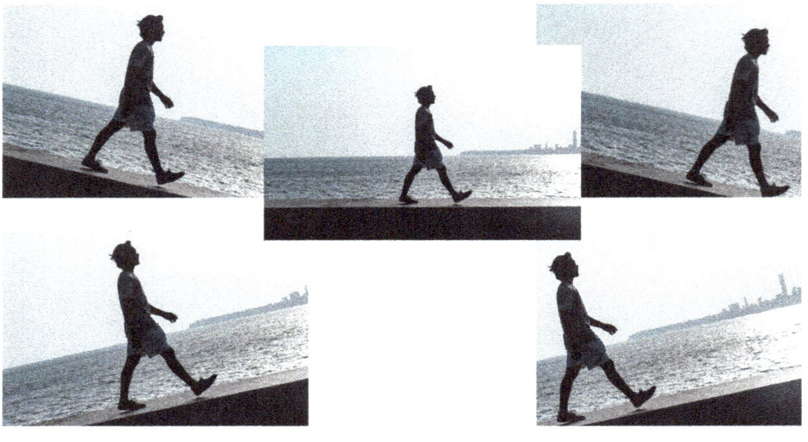

Another example of combining camera and subject positions is

Dutching. Notice how the placement of the person walking in the frame makes them look stable, walking into open space or as if they are about to fall out of the frame.

Step 2 wants you to consider minor adjustments to the camera position to reframe the subject. You could also reposition your subject.

How does the eye work?

The retina at the back of our eye has photoreceptor cells that process the world in front of us. These photoreceptor cells are densely packed in a small area known as the fovea. The fovea is the center of our vision, where we have the highest resolution of visual acuity. Our detailed perception drops from the center of our vision to the periphery (peripheral vision).

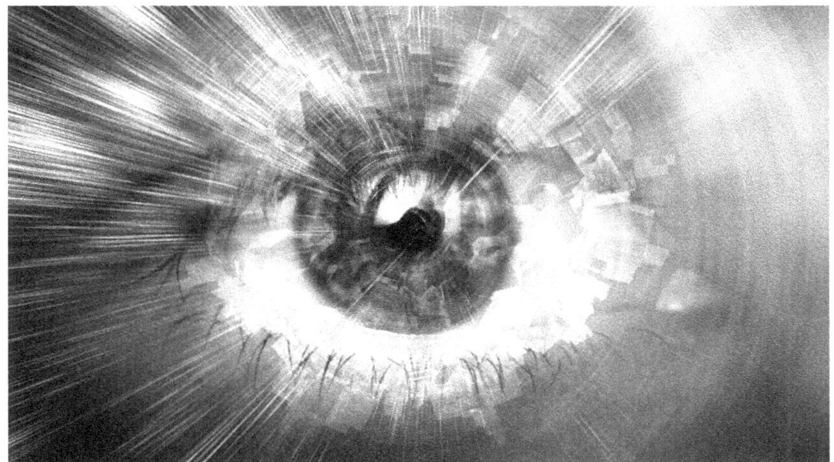

A quick exercise: Stare at the letter X in the next line and, without moving your eyes, try to read the lines of text above and below.

X

Pretty tricky, right? And why am I explaining how our eyes work, anyway? Well, that's a great question!

The previous exercise clearly demonstrates that when we look at a photo, we simply cannot take it all in at once. But, by making your main subject stand out, you're encouraging the viewer to align their fovea (center of focus) to that location. This is called a fixation.

Using the techniques in this section, you are placing the main subject with space around it. This urges the viewer to do a visual search and scan (also known as foveation) to be fixated on again between eye movements.

How cool is that!? Are you geeking out on this like I am? Yes... No? Ok, let's move on then...

Remember: Not all photos need to include a subject. They just need a starting point (visual anchor) to engage the viewer.

Visual anchor - where the eye lands

Not every photo needs to have an anchor, but it certainly helps to have a point of fixation to create an engaging photo.

You should include one main area or subject/focal point to attract viewers' eyes and engage them. That focal point can be a single subject, a foreground interest, a gesture, a single color or texture.

How do we achieve this? First, ask yourself these questions: Is the main subject/area in focus, well-lit, sharp, or colourful?

If your subject is a person or animal, are they making eye contact with the camera or with something else in the photo?

If you can't answer yes to at least one of those questions, consider finding a different focus to better attract viewers.

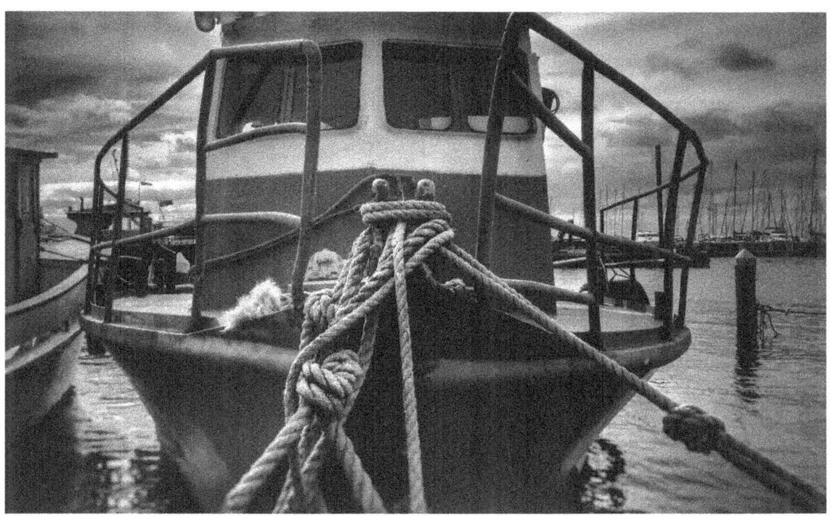

Emphasis - dominance

Similar to a visual anchor, this technique places more visual weight on a particular area in the frame.

The strength of emphasis or dominance that an element has in a photo is determined by multiple factors, such as color, shape, and size.

There are also genre-specific tips we can use to create more emphasis. For example, when looking at a group of people in portrait photography, the closest and largest person will often become the visual anchor. For portrait photography, position your subject as the only one making eye contact with the viewer. This places extra emphasis on the subject while creating a stronger connection with the viewer.

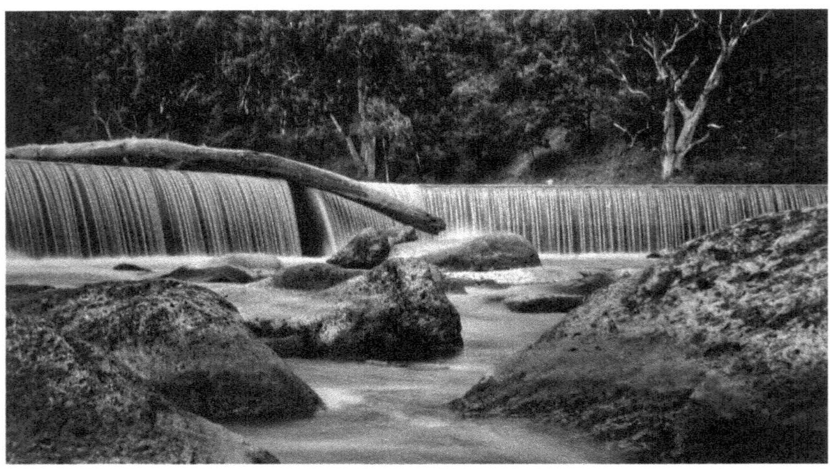

As you review your photo, you may notice that something undesirable has unfortunately dominated the photo. In the example above, the water was originally unpleasantly brown, taking attention away from the textures.

By editing the photo to be monochromatic, I was able to redirect the emphasis and add dominance back to the flowing water's texture.

Off-centre

When the main subject is placed in the center of the frame, the attention of the viewer is attracted immediately to that subject. Yet, it can be hard to shift the viewer's focus to a centered subject. We tend to fixate on the middle of the frame.

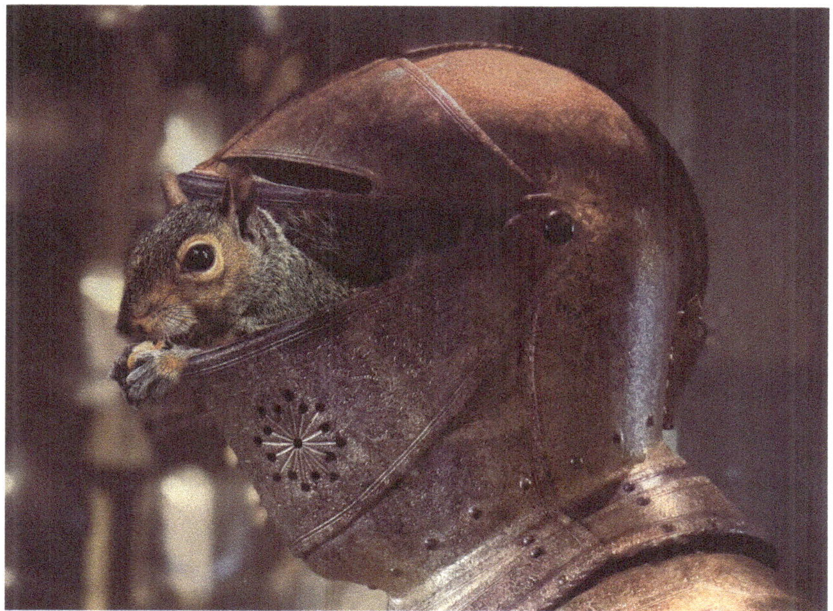

To create space for the viewer, place the subject off-center. This lets them explore after they finish looking at it.

Other elements in the frame, in this instance, become even more essential for providing balance and context to the story in the photo.

Rule of thirds

This popular composition technique is available as an option on most smartphone cameras in the settings, named grid lines or grid. The grid overlay has two vertical and two horizontal lines. They create a nine-square grid, like a tic-tac-toe board. It is the placement of the lines that assists you in placing objects off-center. It is not so much about the nine squares at all.

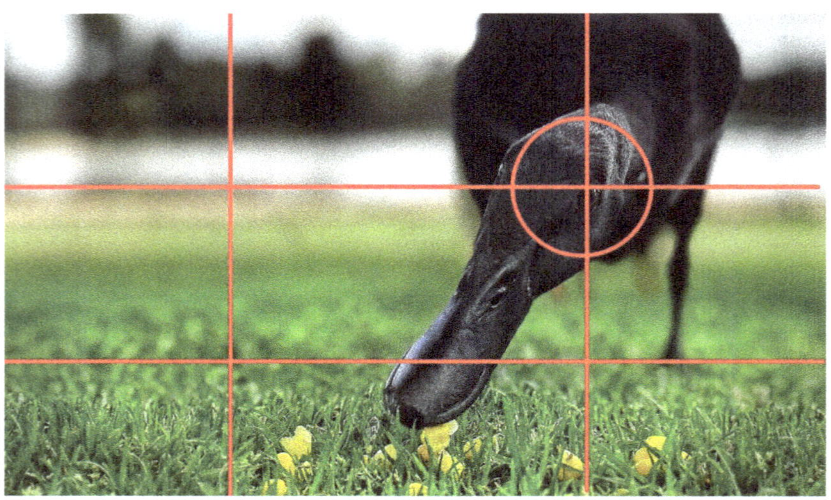

If you place the main subject off-center on one of the intersecting lines, you will have a more dynamic photo.

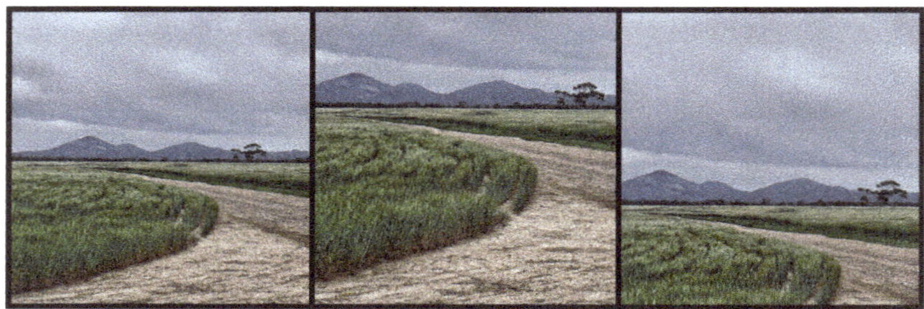

In the above collage, notice that the horizon in the center effectively splits the photo into two equal halves. Moving the horizon fills two-thirds of the frame with the foreground or sky. It makes it clear to the viewer where to focus. If the sky only occupies a small section of the frame, their attention will generally be more attracted to the foreground.

One-third - two-thirds

As an extension of the Rule of Thirds, this technique involves the main subject occupying two-thirds of one of the lines in the grid. Like many composition techniques, this is a combination of two techniques. In this instance, it is the rule of thirds and dominance.

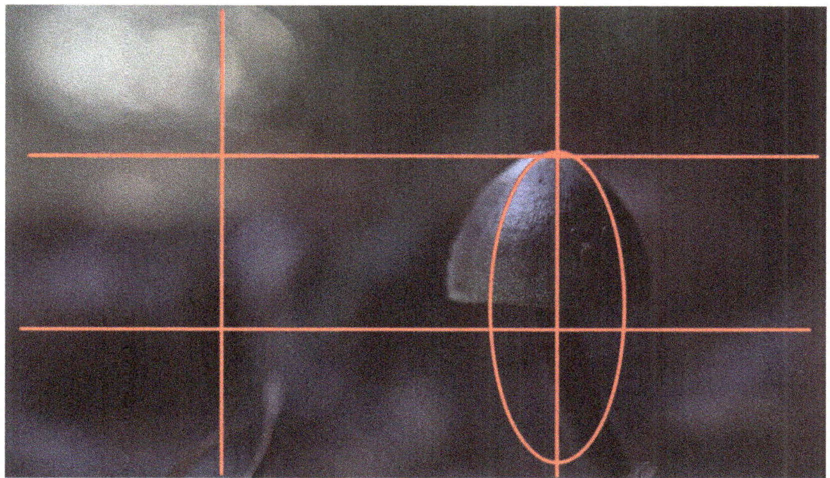

Left to right

The left-to-right compositional technique is based on the viewer reading the photo like a book, reading from left to right. To create harmony in a photo, position elements with more emphasis on the left. This will encourage viewers to focus there.

Like all techniques, how you use this technique is really up to your personal preference and depends on the viewer's experience. And, in this case, culture. If the viewer reads text from right to left, like in certain Asian languages, this technique will not be as effective.

As with almost everything in photography. There is no right and wrong. I ran a poll in my Smartphone Photography Club community on which version of the photo they preferred. The result was a surprising 50:50.

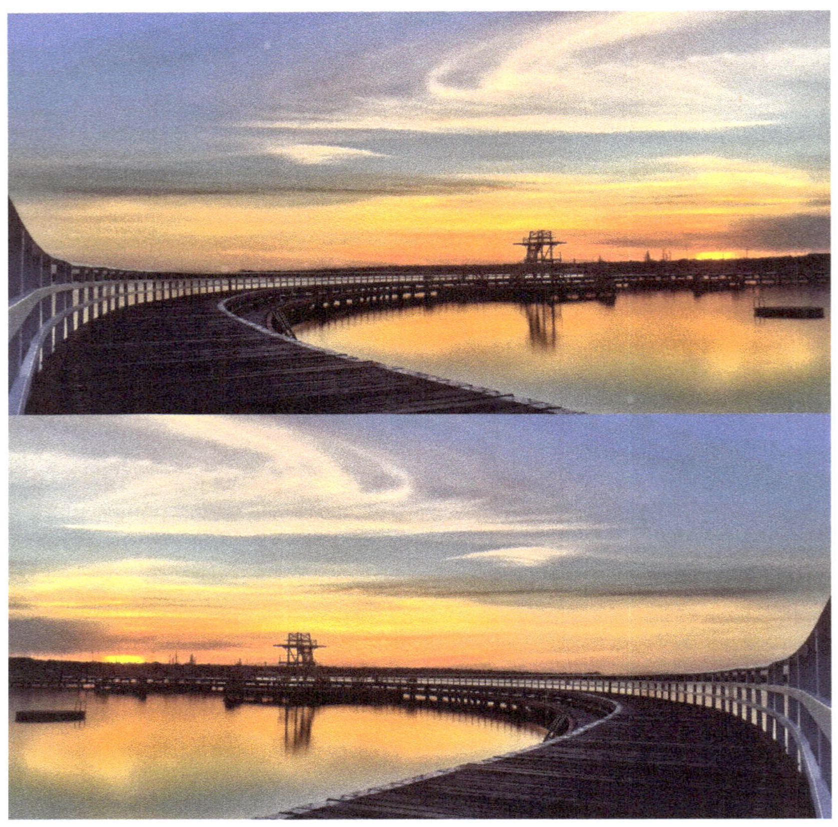

Centred

I may have talked you out of centering a subject after discussing the off-center and the Rule of Thirds techniques. That said, stay with me on this one.

Imagine a simplistic overhead photo of a plate of food on a table. It would look weird or awkward if you were to position the plate off-center with nothing else on the table. In this scenario, you want the viewer to look straight at the center of the frame. You want the viewer to be able to take in the entire visual of the plate's contents, not have their attention diverted by a glass in the corner of the frame.

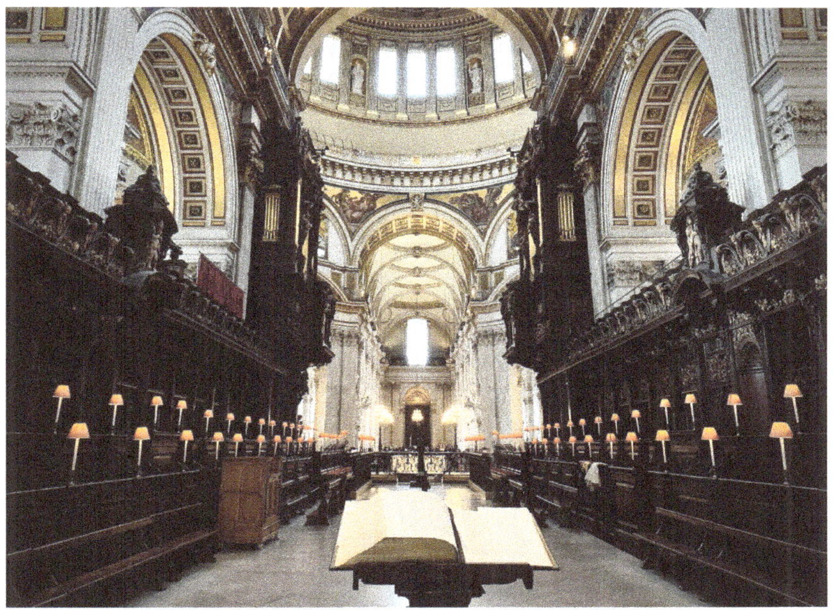

A centered subject may seem like a contradiction, considering the other techniques we've discussed. Yet, it is just as valid a compositional technique as off-center and the rule of thirds. It's your subject, scene, and intention that ultimately will help you determine which technique is best.

Frame within a frame

Also known as sub-framing, the frame-within-a-frame technique is like framing. It creates a border around the subject within the photo itself to attract and maintain your attention. A framed area within a framed photo allows you to maintain viewers' attention within a specific part of the photo.

This technique appears in interior photos with a view through a window. The window frame serves as a sneak peek into the outside world. Take a look at how this creates depth in the photo and provides an opportunity to evoke the viewer's imagination in the example photo below.

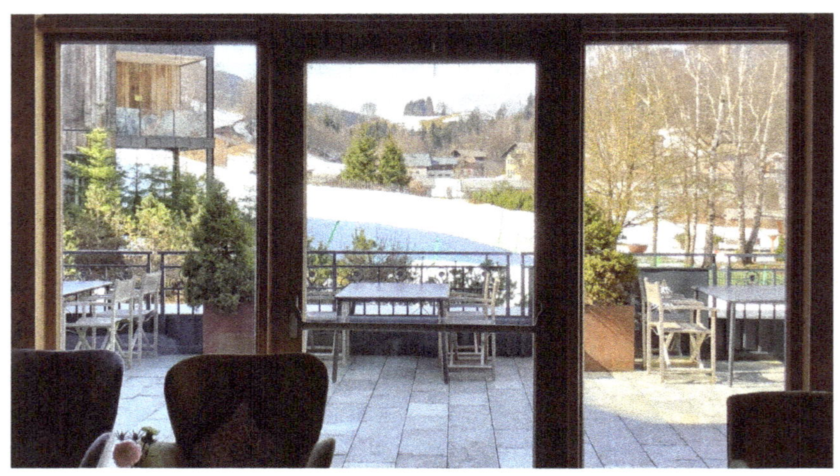

Negative space

There are quite a few compositional tips related to the use of space in relation to the subject and surrounding elements in the frame. Negative space refers to the unoccupied areas around the main subject. If this space is free of distractions, the main subject becomes more isolated and stands out more to the viewer.

The negative space can be a color, a flat surface like a wall, in nature, open spaces like a blurred distant background, or the sky. A distraction-free negative space creates calm. It also emphasizes the main subject. This achieves a pleasing aesthetic. A busy, content-filled negative space can overwhelm the subject. It adds energy and creates visual tension.

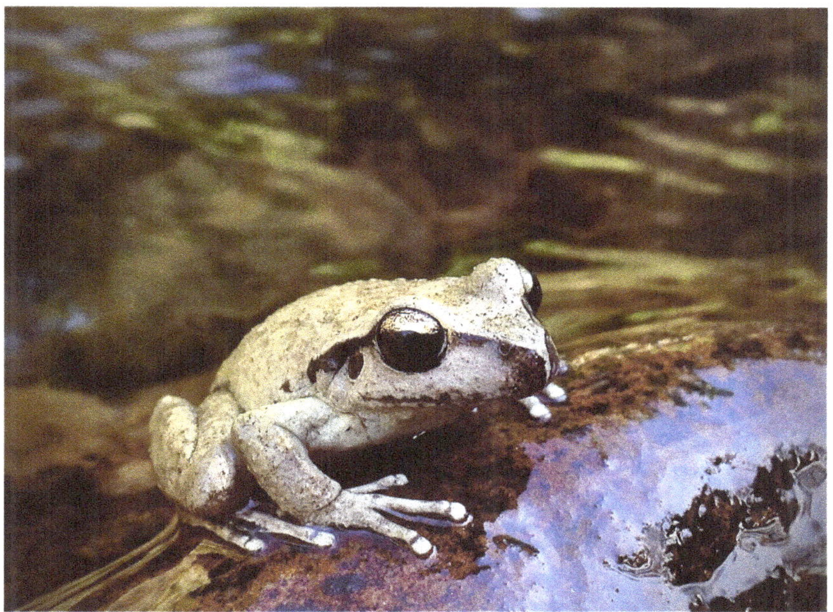

Positive space

As we've discussed, negative space is the area outside of the subject. So, let's now get into its opposite, positive space. Positive space is the area the main subject occupies. It could be a person, an animal, a building, or a flower; as long as it captures the viewer's attention when they look at the photo, almost anything is acceptable.

Active space

Negative space separates the subject from other elements in the frame. Active space is the part of that negative space. It is weighted toward the direction the main subject is travelling.

Active space is also referred to as giving the subject room to "move into." Leaving space in front of your subject encourages viewers to look there. It also creates a sense of where the subject is going.

In contrast, if the subject is at the edge of the frame and moving outwards, it creates visual tension for the viewer. The mystery of not knowing what is ahead of the subject can make it feel like an imminent collision. This visual tension can make the viewer feel claustrophobic.

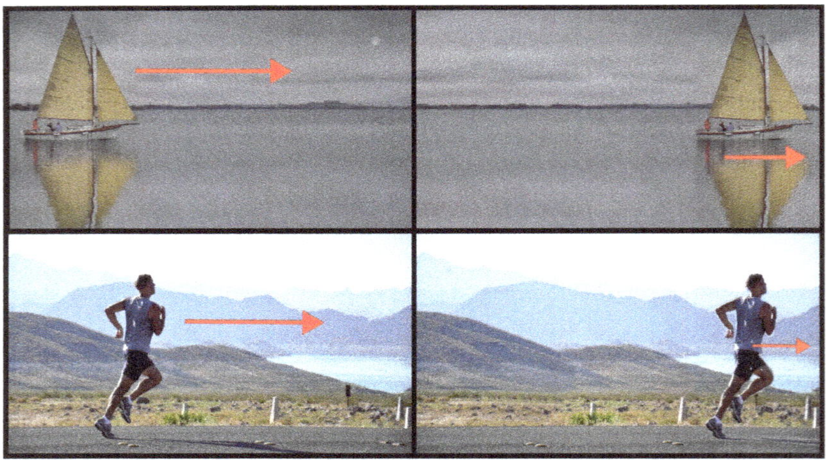

Repetition and pattern

Repetition is when an object repeats, recurring in a photo. Keep in mind that although the object repeats, it can still form another shape or slightly change in another way.

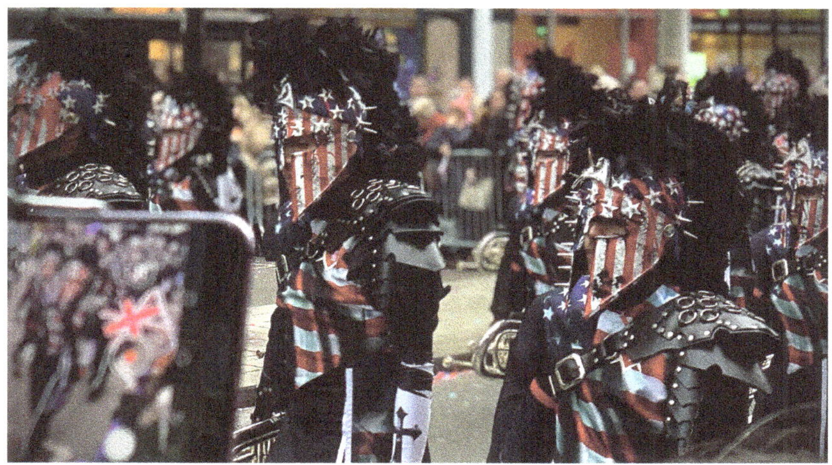

Different from repetition, patterns occur when a few different objects are repeated and changed. Repetition and patterns are all about repeating elements.

Isolation

Isolation occurs when your subject stands out in a photo by itself, pulling the viewer's attention. One of the easiest capture techniques for this method is shooting at a low angle where the background behind the subject is the sky.

Another way you can isolate the subject is to create separation from the background. This can include a contrasting, blurred, or muted background. All are designed to focus attention on the subject.

Avoid mergers

Later, we'll talk about the benefits of overlapping elements, but for now, let's talk about how to avoid mergers. When photographing silhouettes, overlapping elements merge. This ruins your shapes' outlines. The secret to a great silhouette is to avoid critical focal points touching or interfering with each other.

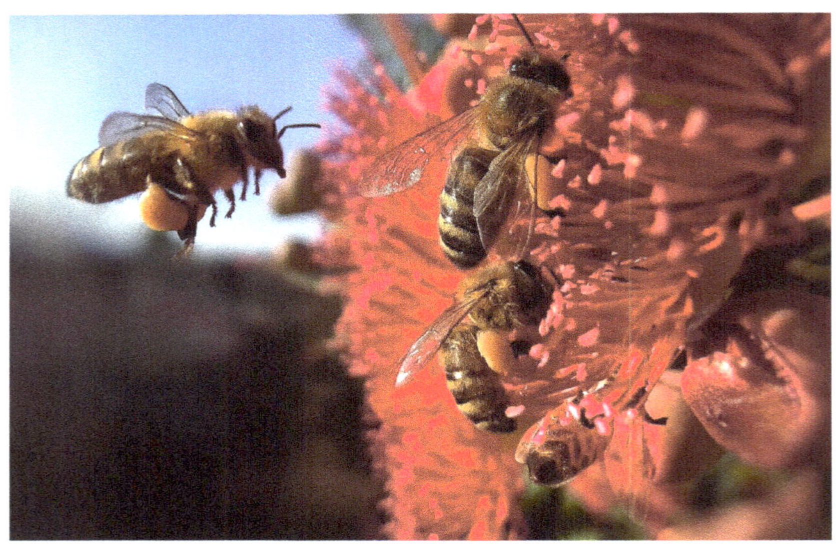

Fill the frame

Filling the frame is what it sounds like. It is when your subject takes up most of the frame. This can be handy if the background is undesirable and you don't have the luxury of changing angles.

When filling the frame, be aware that digital zoom will degrade your photo, and cropping will reduce the number of pixels. Also, be mindful that you may introduce some lens-to-subject distance distortion if you get too close to the subject.

Tip: Use the 2x telephoto (or lens attachment) to get in close and avoid distortion.

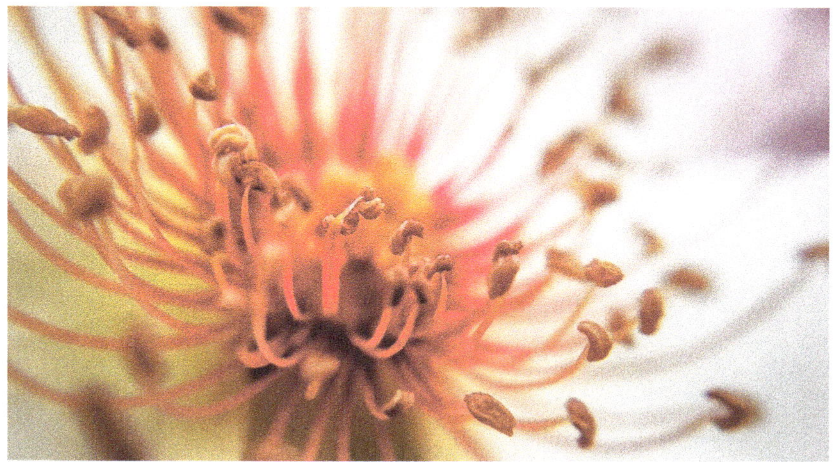

Some genres of photography, in particular, benefit immensely from filling the frame. Sports and street photography often portray a moment of action or a gesture that can be lost if it only takes up a small part of the frame. By zooming in or cropping in editing, you can bring that gesture or moment to the attention of the viewer more intensely.

You may have heard the phrase 'If it's not good enough, it's not close enough.'

Proportion

Like the earlier-mentioned visual anchor, you can also use proportion to attract viewers' attention. So, use it like the emphasis and dominance techniques. Proportion is the size of an element relative to other elements and the frame as a whole.

Another way to use proportion is to include elements with abnormal proportions. This can introduce visual tension and create a sense of whimsy and humor that further engages the viewer.

Silhouette

A silhouette occurs when you backlight your subject. It creates a shadowy outline and removes details from the subject. Silhouettes convey mystery and drama and can foster a strong emotional connection with your audience. Silhouettes tell simple, distraction-free stories. They are easy for viewers to interpret. The absence of detail allows our imaginations to jump in, transporting us, as viewers, to that moment or location.

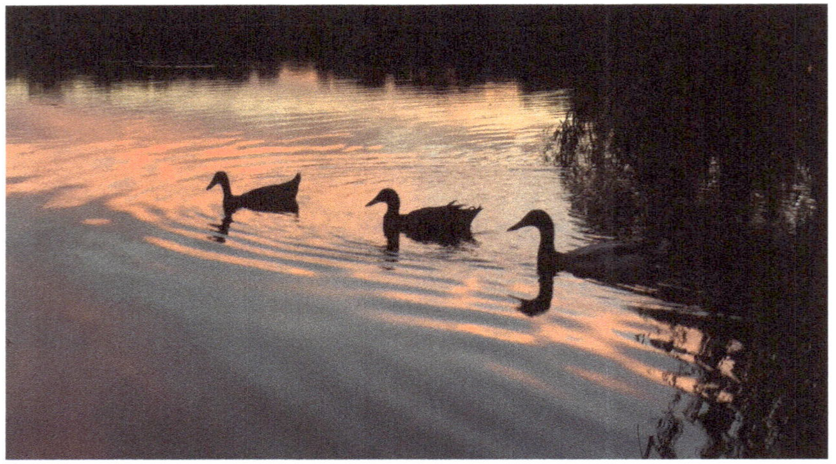

Juxtaposition - colours/tones/textures

Juxtaposition is all about visual contrast (the contrast between two things). I've split the juxtaposition into two sections. This ensures a full understanding of the differences between colour/tones and time/objects.

The simplest definition of juxtaposition is an element that stands out against the background. You can create this separation by isolating or contrasting: colors, tones, textures, shapes, alignments, directions, heights, and sizes.

Later, we will explore contrast in more detail. For now, contrast is the difference between two things. A strong contrast makes the difference between two things clear. It makes one stand out more than the other.

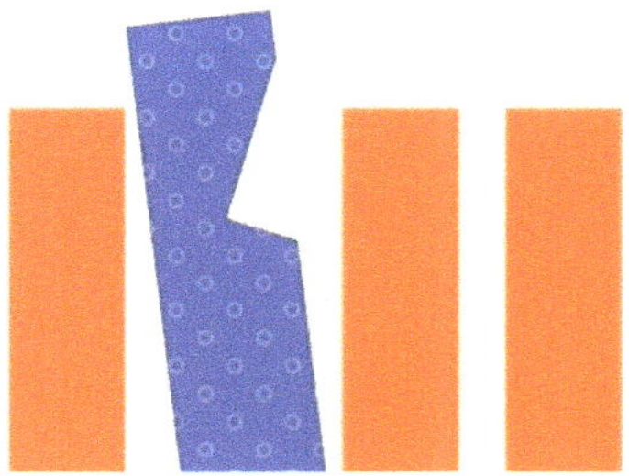

Below are two examples of detailed branches set against a smooth background. This creates a contrast. In each example, I inverted the colors to demonstrate how much stronger the contrast is in the second photo.

The color contrast makes the flowers more engaging and draws the viewers' attention. You can identify contrast by inverting the colors of your photo in editing or squinting your eyes when you're out capturing photos. Squinting helps isolate bright areas in the scene in front of you.

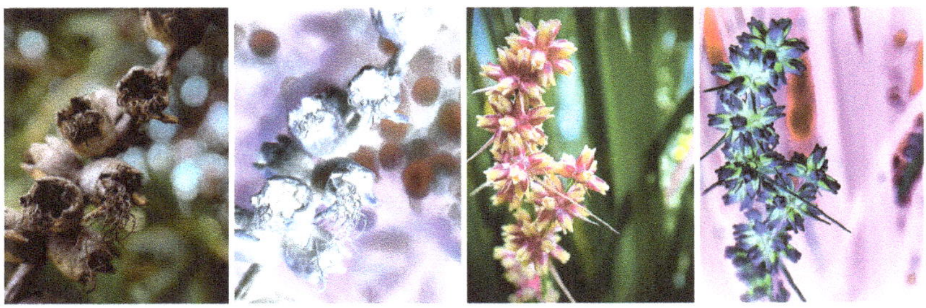

Juxtaposition - time/objects

Juxtaposition requires placing two things next to each other to show the differences between them. This contrast in a photo makes it more fascinating and helps the viewer's eye find the visual anchor.

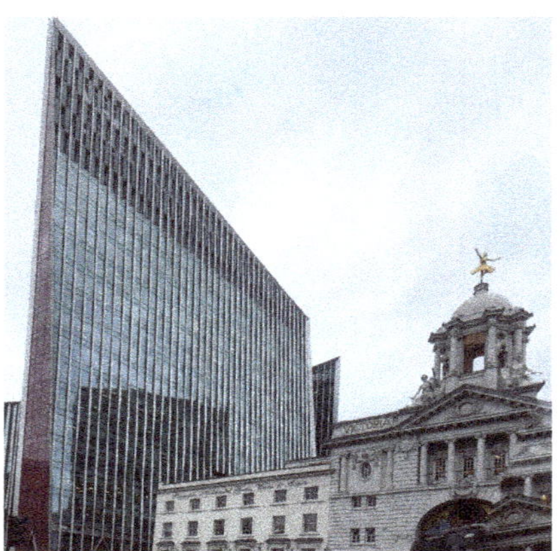

One of my favorite juxtapositions to depict is that of something old and something new.

This could be an old person with a young one, a freshly bloomed flower among dead leaves, or a smartphone on a handwritten letter.

Every time I see a new building erected amongst old buildings, it's like a visual magnet, and I become mesmerized. I love the respect for preserving heritage working in tandem with modern materials and design to either complement existing structures or completely juxtapose them.

Eye contact

I didn't want to include posing and other genre-specific composition tools. So, as you learn about this compositional technique, I'd like you to please keep in mind that it extends to most genres, not just portraits. You can apply eye contact as a technique with inanimate objects by positioning them to face the viewer.

It is in our nature to notice things looking at us and to look for faces, or other recognizable features, in the things we see. It is said to be a survival instinct and may explain why many of us are so good at reading expressions and intentions in facial features.

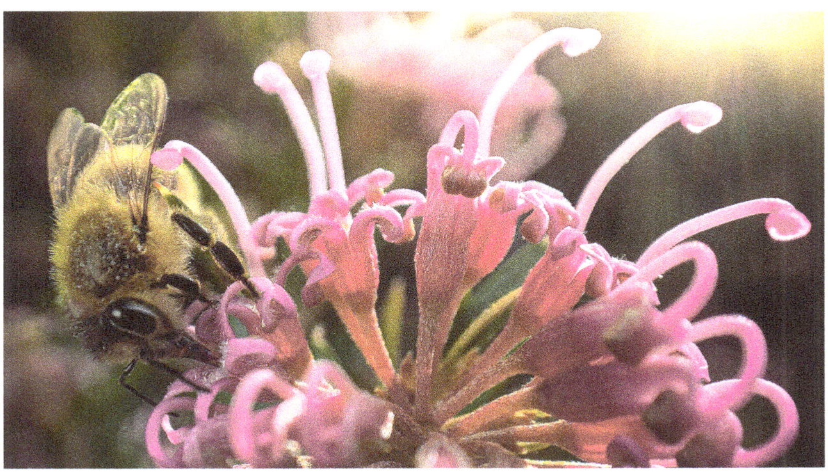

You may have heard the saying that the eyes are the gateway to the soul. It may be cliché, but clichés exist for a reason. And making eye contact with the subject definitely establishes a connection with the viewer.

Take a look at the above photo comparison showing a bee moving around a flower. Which would appeal to you more, the bee showing its compound eye or its back?

Step 2 - list of techniques

How does the eye work?	Active space
Visual anchor	Repetition and pattern
Emphasis - dominance	Isolation
Off-centre	Avoid mergers
Rule of thirds	Fill the frame
One-third - two-thirds	Proportion
Left to right	Silhouette
Centred	Juxtaposition - colours/tones
Frame within a frame	Juxtaposition - time/objects
Negative space	Eye contact
Positive space	

STEP 3: Position the Contextual Elements

Step 3 is about taking in the entire scene in front of us and deconstructing it into separate elements. This section will look at the placement of supporting elements and how they interact with the main subject.

Using Gestalt Theory (German for shape) from the 1920s, we'll discuss visual perception principles. They explain how the brain processes unordered photos.

What are elements?

Elements are any items in the photo's frame. They include the subject and background. They provide context for the photo's location, time, activity, and mood. The narrative in a photo is determined by more than just the inclusion of elements; it's also how and why those elements interact with each other.

Elements are more than just stuff in the photo

Have you ever come across a group of people on the street looking up at something? Did you give in to the temptation to look up to see what they were looking at? If you were to capture this moment in a photo, this gesture would create an implied line of sight. And, just as in reality, we can't help but look across the 2-dimensional photo to see what the subjects are looking at!!

You can better direct the viewer's eye around the photo. Do this by identifying visual elements like line, texture, pattern, diminishing points, scale, and color. This is what that elusive storytelling in photography is all about!

Positioning of elements creates balance

Balance can be created or found in the equal distribution of visual weight across all elements in a given frame. And, as we've discussed, visual weight refers to the amount of impact or force that an element has in a picture. Visual weight measures how much an element attracts viewers. It depends on factors like color, shape, and size.

Remember: Our goal is to construct a photo creatively, cohesively, and with our intention in mind.

While you want to use multiple elements to improve your photos, this is not a test of mashing together composition techniques. This is merely a list of elements to be considered.

Alright, let's get into some of the individual elements (components) of a photo that you can incorporate into your photography.

Closure

We've covered how our eye has a central part in focus and then periphery vision. Our eyes and brains work together to see details and make sense of them! Our brain is quite capable of filling in gaps to complete the missing pieces.

Closure is how our brain fills in the gaps when a road exits one side of the frame and re-enters further along the same edge. As we observe the photo, our brain tracks along the outside of the frame, filling in the blank.

Photos with fog, dark shadows, or other areas that are void of information can create a sense of mystery. It makes the viewer question, "What's there? Who are they? What are they doing?"

Take the photo below as an example. The puddle gives the photo a sense of mystery by covering parts of the scene. It allows the viewer an opportunity to fill in the visual gaps in the photo, complete it and find closure for themselves.

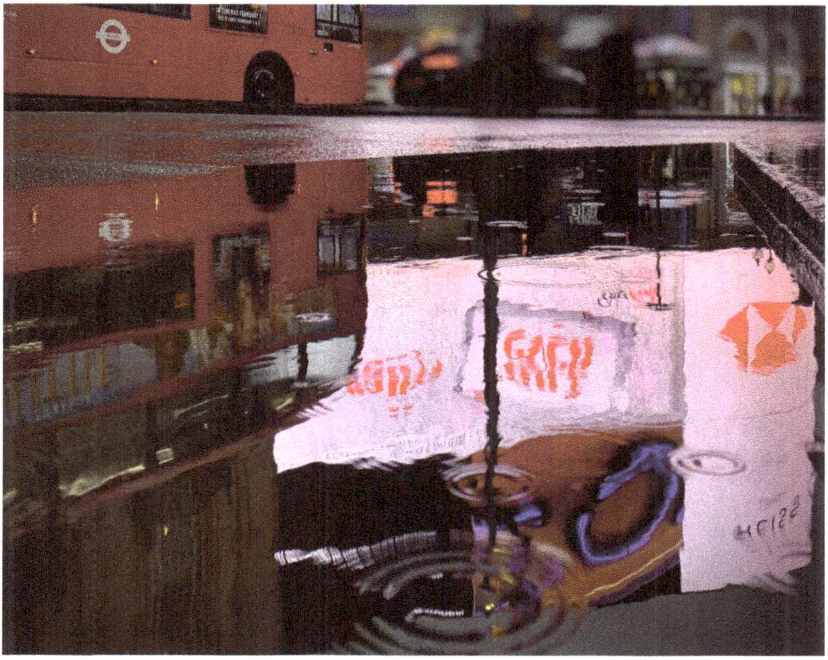

We're most capable of engaging audiences when they can create their visual narrative. As photographers, we must give enough visual clues to provide context. This will encourage viewers to use their imagination to fill in the gaps.

Figure to ground - context

In a photo, we instinctively simplify the scene. We want to find the main subject (figure) and the background (ground). They refer to this relationship between the two as the figure-to-ground relationship.

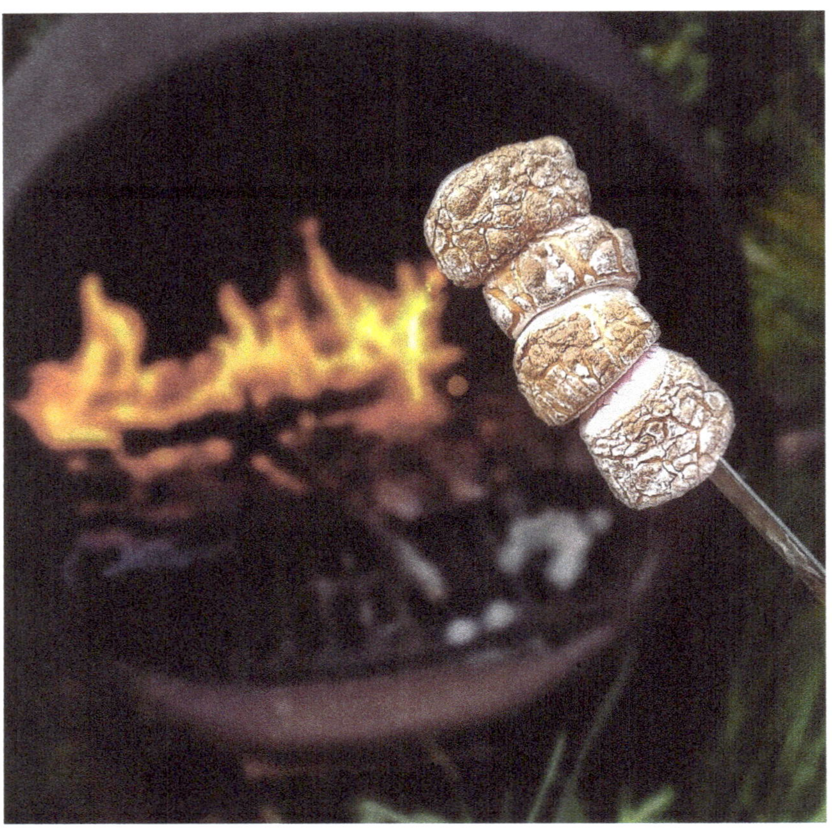

An unstable figure-to-ground relationship makes it hard to see the main subject against the background. Photos that use this technique make viewers question the subject and background. This can even spark debates among them! An object or area in the photo can grab our attention first as the main subject before our eye is drawn to explore the remaining area of the photo.

In photos, larger, focused, and high-contrast objects stand out more. So do those with vivid colors and those isolated from the background. For example, in the photo, the marshmallows draw more attention than the distant fire. The blur, low contrast, and muted colors cause this.

Proximity - unity and abundance

Proximity is how close or far apart certain things are in a photo. It requires you to consider the positioning of elements within a group instead of viewing them individually. You can use proximity, a compositional technique, to group or isolate elements. This can create balance or visual tension. It is intricately connected to the positive and negative space techniques.

Grouping objects and elements together creates unity. They are less likely to seem like random items in a photo. Imagine a garden spilling over with lush, vibrantly colored flowers (abundance). This works well, so long as it's contained and doesn't become overly distracting.

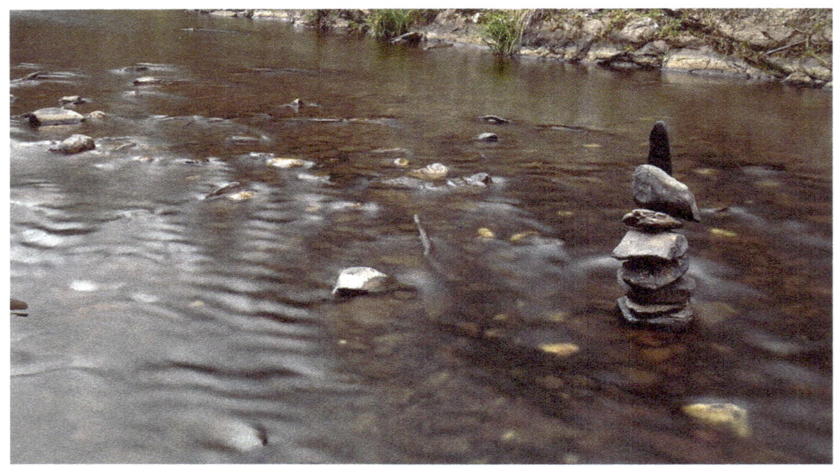

Objects and elements positioned close together in a group create unity and are less likely to look like unrelated, randomized items in a photo. Imagine a garden spilling over with lush, vibrantly coloured flowers (abundance). This works well, so long as it's contained and doesn't become overly distracting.

Common fate

Like the law of proximity covered before, we perceive objects in a scene that are oriented in the same direction as one coherent group. It doesn't matter where they are in the photo. If they all look the same way, we see them as one connected element.

A herd of sheep walking in the same direction, even though there may be different colored sheep, are all still seen as a group. A common fate of walking in the same direction is a strong visual cue. It occurs before we recognize the sheep as separate beings.

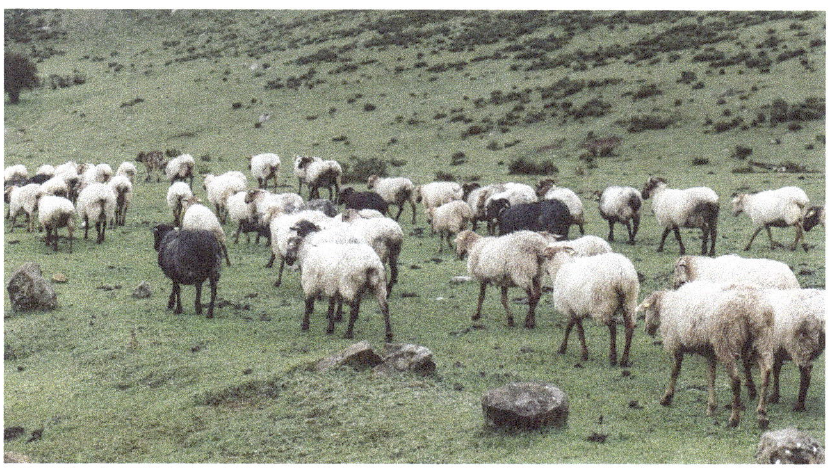

How do we apply this? In short, patience. Sometimes, you may have to wait for a group of animals to orientate themselves in unison to achieve a more pleasing photo.

To capture an odd animal, you can try using isolation and contrast against the common fate. There is no right and wrong way to capture a herd of animals. This is one tool to consider and a reminder that elements that appear to move in the same direction create a theme in your photo.

Continuance

The Law of Continuance states that if a scene's elements follow a continuous visual path, the viewer will assume they extend along it. This can be beyond the edges of the photo or behind some obstruction. It's all about our minds filling in blanks by using our visual system (eyes and brain).

If we cannot see the actual end of the bridge, we imagine that it keeps going. The theory isn't just for paths or roads. It's also for alignment with any sequence, pattern, or grouping of lines or shapes that we can follow.

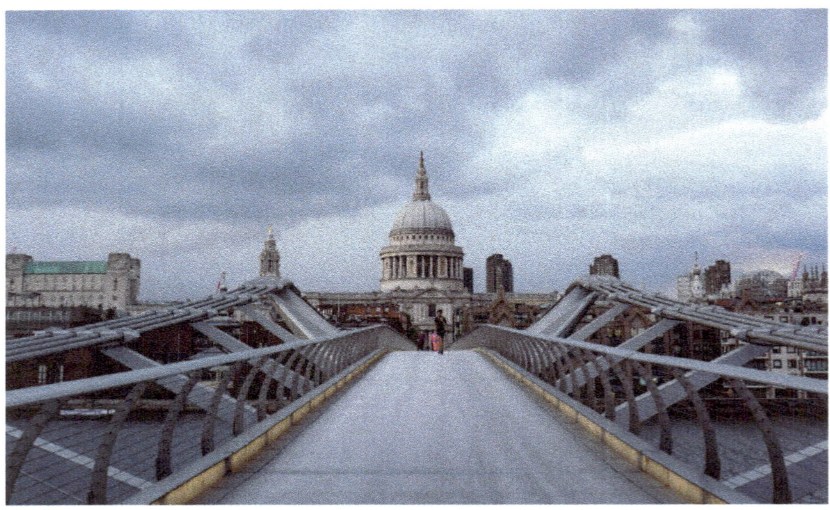

This explains why leading lines are so powerful, as the viewer instinctively follows them to their natural end. Continuance is the key to manipulating viewer attention. It directs their eye movements around the photo, effectively 'reading' your visual story.

Unlike leading lines, continuance doesn't need to have an object or subject at the end to please the viewer. The power, instead, comes from having the viewer fill in the blanks of what may or may not be unseen.

Similarity

Gestalt's theory includes a principle called the Law of Similarity. It says our brains group similar subjects together. When a group of flowers or animals faces different directions, we tend to associate the few that face the same direction as related.

In a busy photo, if many items share an attribute, the viewer will group them. The shared feature will be a unifying factor.

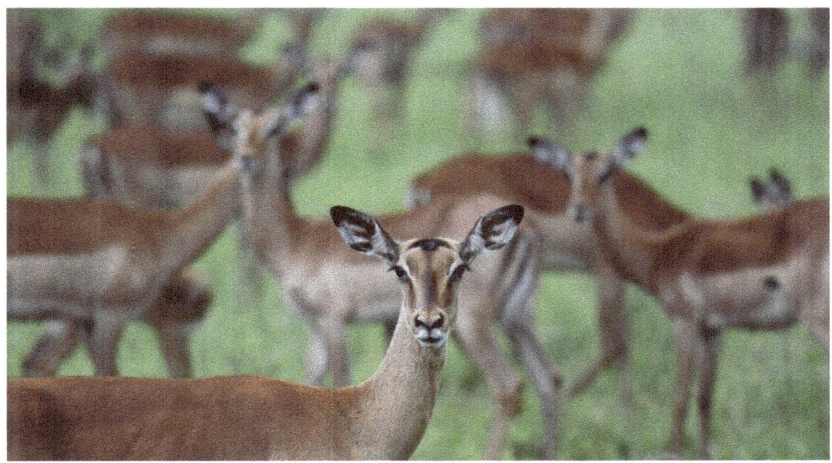

The Gestalt Law of Similarity explores the brain's urge to find meaning in matching features. Our goal in photo composition is to help the viewer make those connections more effectively.

Minimalism

Photography is largely subtractive and requires the removal of objects that don't add value to the photo. Minimalism in photography means using the least amount of content possible to communicate the story in your photo.

Some genres lend themselves to minimalism better than others. For example, this is an excellent technique for architectural subjects to showcase lines, textures, and forms. To take a minimalistic photo of a building, use a wide-angle lens in landscape mode. It will capture everything (near and distant) in a wide view.

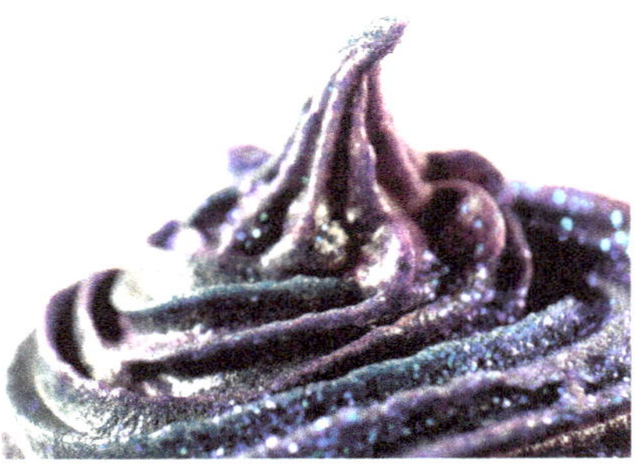

Tip: Editing a high-contrast photo to be black and white, with few mid-tones, can create a more minimalistic look. It reduces details and textures. Creating completely black or white areas makes the scene more straightforward.

Scale - visual cues to emphasise the size

Photographs are two-dimensional. To add depth, they need dimensionality. If that's not a real word, you know what I mean! Introducing elements of a commonly known size enables the viewer to make comparisons with other elements in the frame.

Adding a human element to a landscape is a surefire way to provide scale... we all know the size of a human! Without a scale, one can lose the grandeur of large mountains.

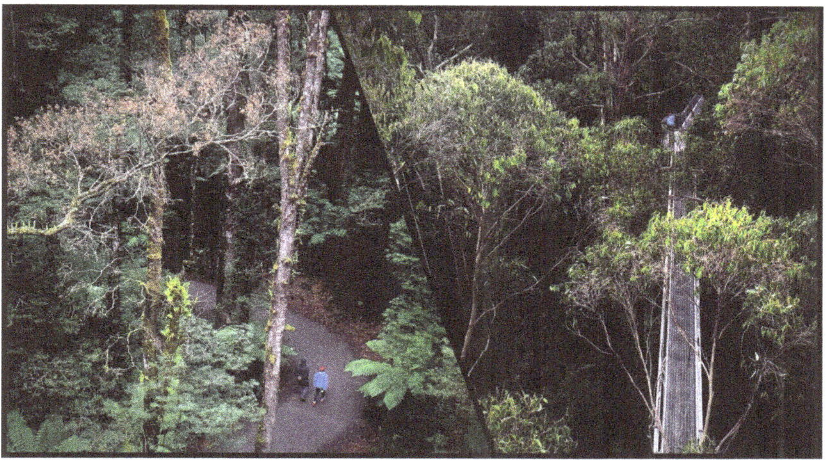

Tip: When adding a human element to the scene, have them wear bright clothing colors that contrast with the scene.

Lines - leading regulating lines

Leading lines are lines within a photo that move the viewer's attention through the photo to a specific element that you want the viewer to notice. In garden design, designers call a leading line a regulating line. It can guide through elements in the frame or to a single element in it.

Leading lines can be actual lines, such as edges of structures or objects, or inferred lines like the tops of trees or buildings. To create a stronger composition, try to identify many leading lines that intersect with the subject.

Tip: A large or bright element at the start of the line encourages the viewer to read it in the intended direction.

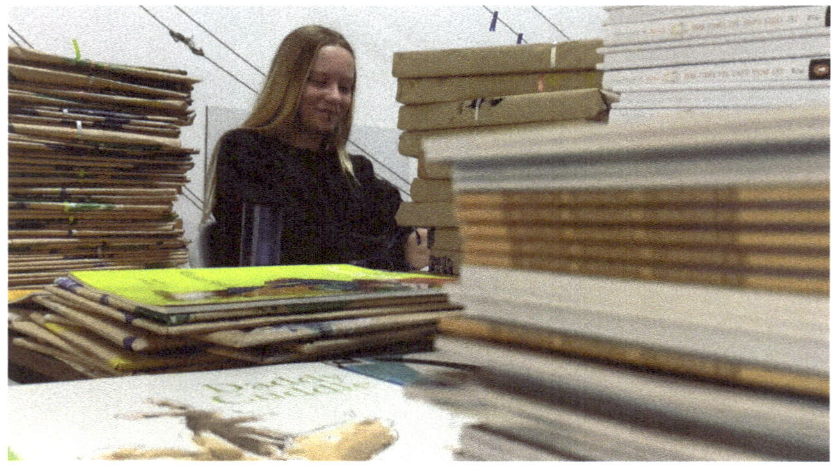

Lines - baroque and sinister diagonal lines

Diagonal lines have a similar effect to leading lines. A diagonal line is a straight line (or an alignment of objects that resemble a line) that travels across the photo to the opposite diagonal corner. A diagonal line encourages the viewer to take more interest and peruse more of the photo.

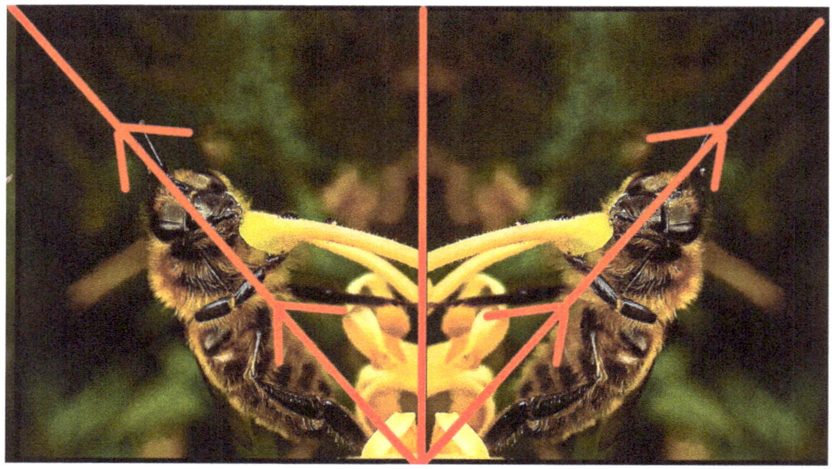

A 'baroque diagonal' refers to a diagonal that traverses from left to right. A diagonal line that runs from right to left is a 'sinister diagonal.' It's the opposite of a baroque diagonal. In some photos, a sinister diagonal can create more visual tension for the viewer.

Imagine walking out your front door at home. How do your eyes scan for dangers? We look down to avoid tripping and then look up scanning from left to right. We naturally scan from bottom left to top right.

Lines - expressive s-curve and z-curves

You can also use S-curved and zigzag lines to encourage and direct viewers' attention through the photo, like a leading line. The technique breaks and interrupts the leading line. It guides the viewer's attention from side to side, swerving through the photo.

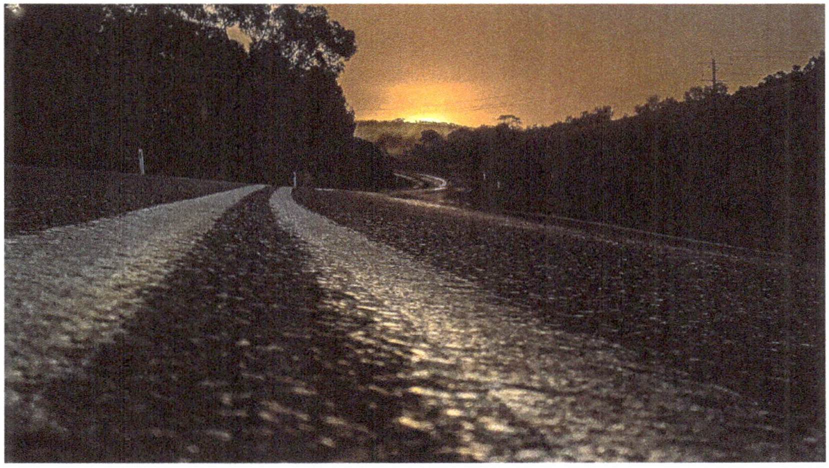

You can also use S-curved and zigzag lines to encourage and direct viewers' attention through the photo, like a leading line. This technique breaks and interrupts the leading line. It guides the viewer's attention from side to side, swerving through the photo.

Lines - horizontal lines (create a plane)

The most commonly referenced leading line that runs from left to right is the horizon. This visible line is what separates the land and sky, providing depth in our natural vision, as well as in photography. Although horizontal lines are static and less dynamic than S-curves and Z-curves, they can create a sense of stability and calm.

As before mentioned, I don't recommend placing the horizon in the centre of the frame. This effectively divides the photo in half and can leave the viewer unsure if the emphasis is on the sky or the ground.

Notice in the photo below all the horizontal lines. The distance between them creates distance references of depth.

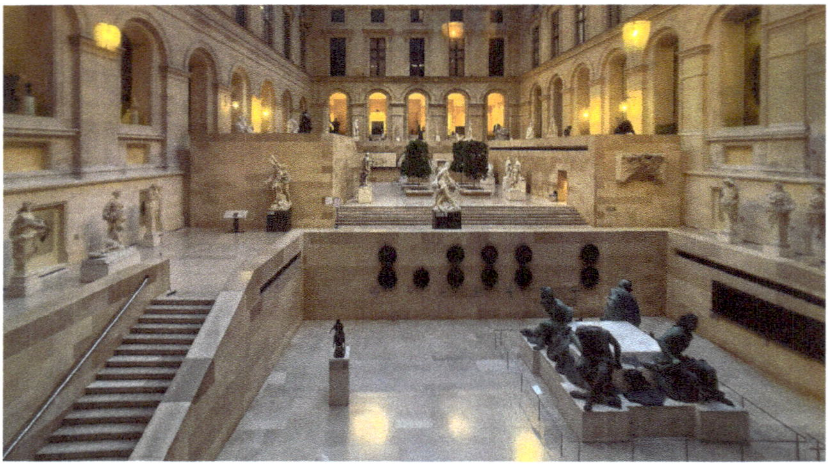

An interesting way you can make use of horizon lines without becoming static or boring is to intersect them with other elements. You can achieve this with a silhouetted element breaking up the line or a leading line merging into and/or through the horizon lines.

Lines - vertical lines (creates stability)

So far, we've covered leading lines and curved lines that engage the viewer and guide them from the visual anchor point to various focal points. We've also discussed how horizontal lines, especially the use of many lines, can provide depth.

I listed vertical lines last. In most English-speaking countries, we read photos from left to right, like text. Our eyes are pre-conditioned to this. This enables us to recognize horizontal lines and deviations along curved lines with ease. But, it also means that vertical lines are often overlooked and can recede into the background.

That said, if a light pole that we know should be vertical is typically leaning over, we notice it. The viewer may notice it without being aware. They might feel something is 'off' with the photo but can't identify why.

Vertical lines of identical elements that recede into the distance and reduce in size, as shown in the photo, can create a sense of depth.

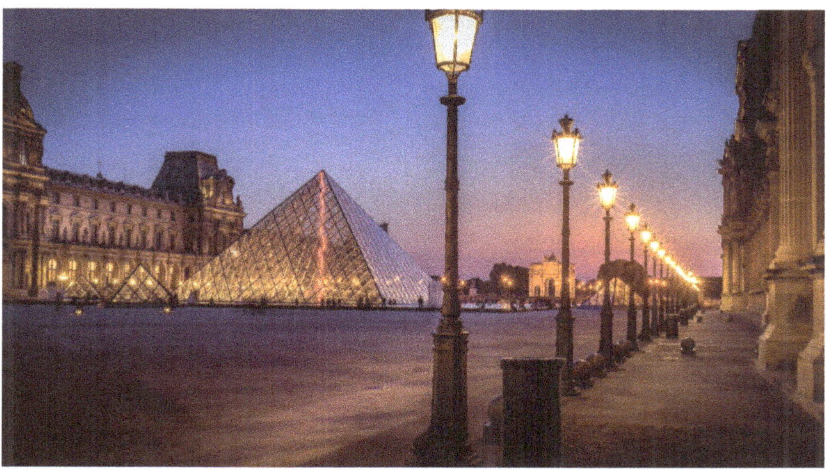

Line - implied line of sight

Implied means a suggestion that is not directly or implicitly expressed. Hence, an implied line of sight is one that you suggest to the viewer through the positioning of your subject and/or supporting elements.

We can create that same urge in our photos by capturing a person, animal, or insect looking across the frame. For example, a photo of a photographer pointing their camera creates a line back to the main focal points of the composition.

Lines - converging lines - vanishing point

This concept has many names: vanishing point, diminishing point, converging lines, point of convergence, and single-point linear perspective. And, I'd wager that you're already familiar with it.

Have you seen any photos of train tracks that converge in the distance? Then, you've seen the vanishing point, the spot to which the receding parallel lines diminish and appear to join. Converging lines are a versatile compositional tool. They create depth and a 3D look. Converging lines, as seen below... can be vertical and horizontal.

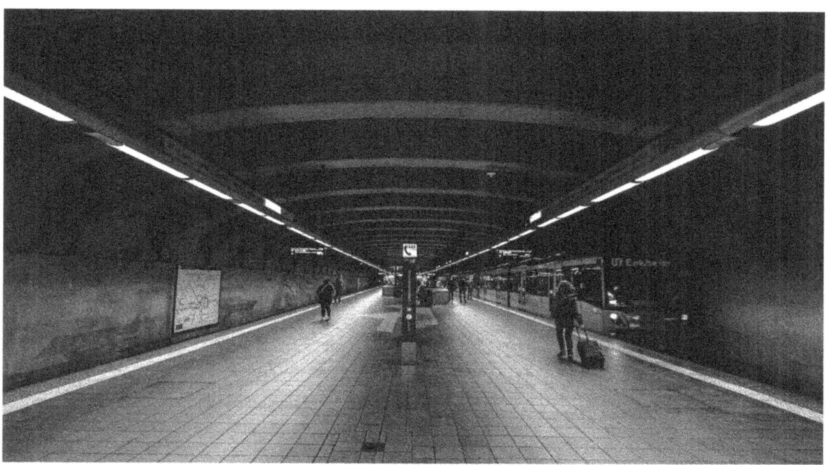

One way to observe the point of convergence in everyday life is to stand in the middle of an empty road. The centre line will continue as far as you can see, but the sides of the road will converge in the distance.

To capture this technique in your photography, the basic ingredients you'll need are two parallel lines and a distant vanishing point.

Triangles

First, this technique is not about geometric shapes in the photo. Instead, the implication suggests the triangle. This technique needs three outer lines of shapes or three elements. They must be arranged to form an implied triangle. You can also use one or two physical lines within the frame (i.e. rooflines, arms, etc.) and an implied line to complete the triangle shape.

Two lines can converge to form an arrow. It directs the viewer's attention. You can also create many triangles with points and lines in one photo!

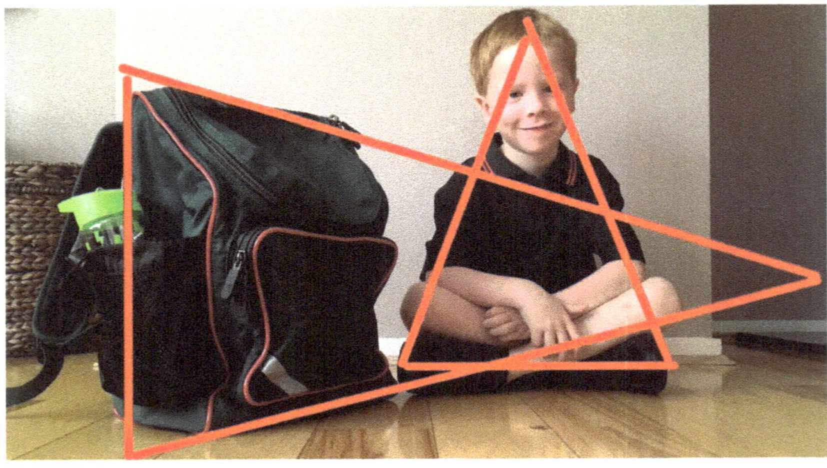

Tip: If the base of your triangle is at the bottom of your photo and the apex is at the top, the photo feels more stable than an inverted triangle.

Golden ratio

Before we explore the phi grid and golden spiral, we first need to cover the golden ratio. The golden ratio is a proportion valued for its beauty. The Greeks named it 'Phi' for the sculptor Phidias, and it is 1.61803.

Hold onto your hat... it's time to get mathematical!

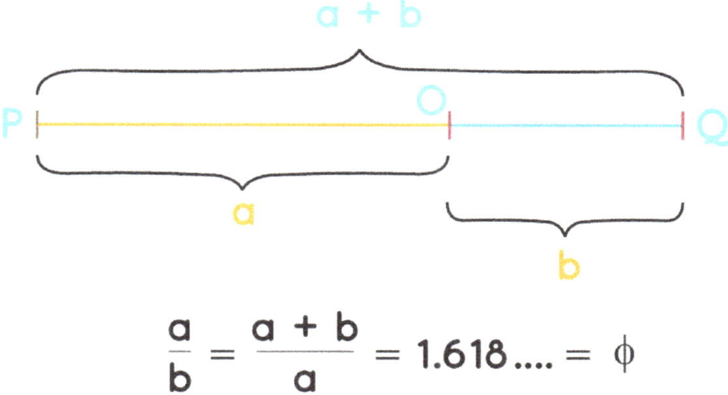

$$\frac{a}{b} = \frac{a + b}{a} = 1.618.... = \phi$$

The golden ratio exists when the ratio of two quantities, relative to each other, equals their sum divided by the larger quantity. The ratio of the length of the longer part "a" to the length of the shorter part "b" is equal to the ratio of their sum "(a + b)" to the longer length.

You do not need to be able to recite or even understand this formula. You can see it everywhere, from the Great Pyramid of Giza (4600 years old) to art. Leonardo Da Vinci referred to the golden ratio as the 'divine proportion'.

As viewers, we are naturally drawn to balance and harmony. As a compositional technique, the golden ratio offers that.

Phi grid

Often confused with The Rule of Thirds, the placement of the grid is spaced according to the golden ratio.

The length of the line is x+y; the first segment is x, and the second segment is y. So the equation is: x/y = (x+y)/x = 1.6180339887498948420

The 'golden ratio' or 'divine proportion' is known as the magical ratio, which is 1.618. In mathematics, it is known as Phi. Photo composition, it's when you place elements, such as the horizon, at the 1.618 positions.

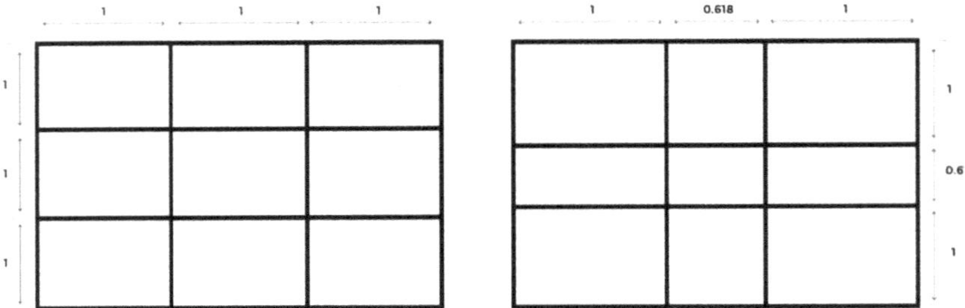

The Rule of Thirds divides the frame into three rows and columns of equal size (1:1:1). The Phi Grid reduces the size of the middle row and middle column to accommodate the golden ratio, resulting in a ratio of 1:1.618:1.

Golden spiral

The golden spiral can work both vertically and horizontally. For this explanation, let's start with a horizontal rectangle.

The golden spiral is a spiral of golden rectangles. Each has a length-to-width ratio of 1.618 (the golden ratio). Each rectangle is larger than the last by a factor of the golden ratio.

The ratio between a horizontal rectangle's length and width is the golden ratio (1.618 aka Phi). Next, partition (split) the rectangle into a square and a leftover rectangle. Notice how it's the same proportions as the first rectangle? This can then be split, again and again, to create the compositional overlay below.

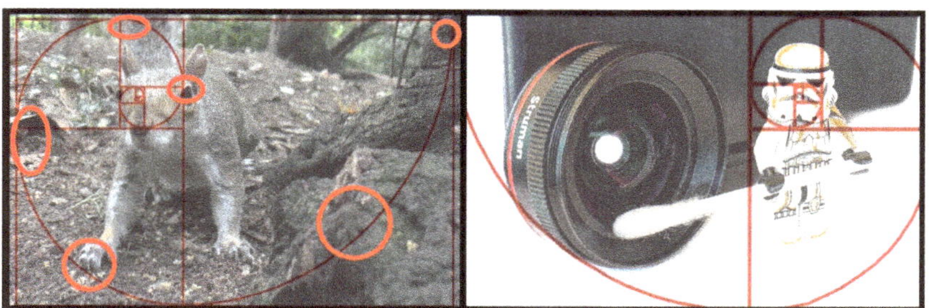

The result is an almost complete partitioning of the rectangle into squares. If you then draw arcs from opposite corners of each square, you'll end up with a curve resembling the shape of a spiral. This curve flows through the frame, leading the viewer's eye around the picture.

Tip: This technique was one of the most difficult for me to understand as a photographer. The secret isn't to position the main subject in the tight circle at the end of the spiral. You also need to include other elements touching the implied spiral as an anchor for the golden spiral. Otherwise, it looks like you placed the main subject off-centre

Fibonacci spiral

The Golden Spiral and Fibonacci Spiral are very similar. In photography, they are indistinguishable. But, before we get into the Fibonacci Spiral, we need to know the Fibonacci sequence. It's a series of numbers found by adding up the two numbers before it:

0, 1, 1, 2, 3, 5, 8, 13, 21, 34, …

The Fibonacci spiral is a spiral of squares. It starts with a 2:1 aspect ratio. The squares increase in size by the Fibonacci sequence.

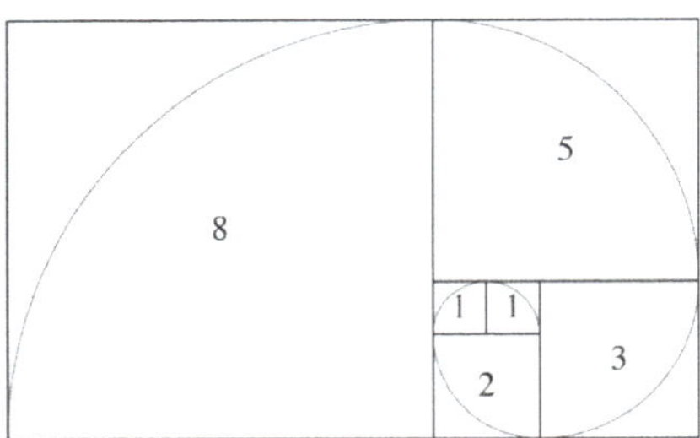

Baroque (golden) diagonal

With this technique, we create a diagonal line (the major line). Then, we add one or more lines from the corner(s) that intersect the diagonal line at a 90-degree angle (the reciprocal line). This then creates triangles with equal ratios, also known as golden.

Like the Rule of Thirds, Baroque diagonal lines serve as a guide for positioning the visual elements in your photographs.

Tip: Outside of these lines, be sure to leave some space for the photo to 'breathe' - remember active space? Why not try to place two focal points on the two intersecting points?

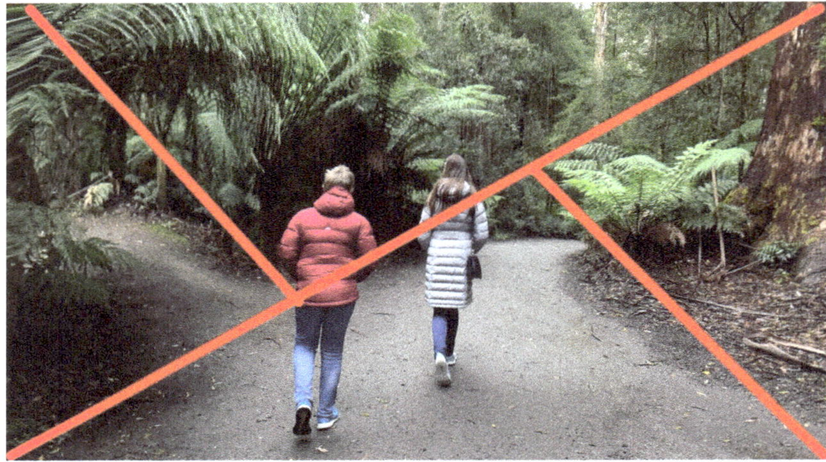

Focal points - hierarchy

No, focal points are *not* related to focus! You're already aware of how important it is to know your photographic intention and motivation for taking a photo. Focal points help you identify the main subject and which elements in the photo you want the viewer to notice. You want the subject and elements to be noticed in a specific order, which is called hierarchy. Both focal points and the visual hierarchy are vital in communicating your intention and motivation to the audience.

In Step 2. we covered Visual Anchor and Emphasis. As a refresher, a visual anchor is the focal point with the most visual weight and is emphasized through various techniques.

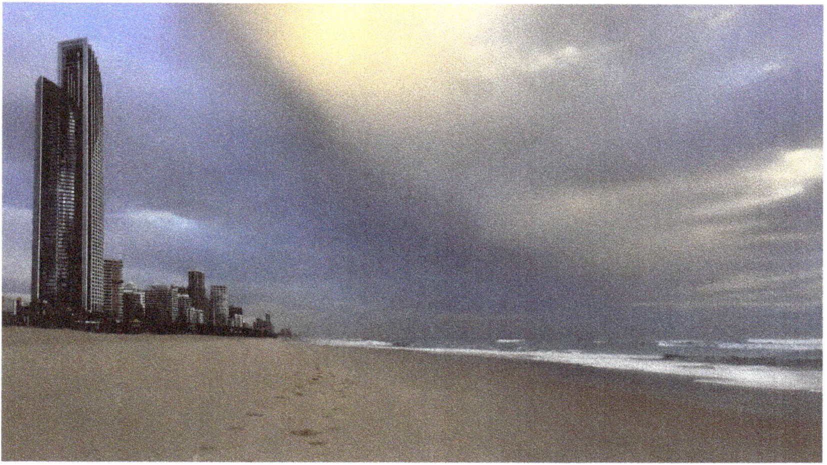

Focal points are the many areas of interest that we want the viewer to notice and move their attention between. A focal point can be a line, shape, form, texture, lighting source, or another element that contextualizes the scene.

Look away from this book before returning your attention to the above photo. Which element did you notice first, second and third? Can you explain why you noticed them in that order?

Foreground interest

A foreground interest element is commonly placed at the bottom of the frame. It can take many shapes and forms and allows you to capture the viewer's attention while encouraging them to look beyond.

The foreground interest does not need to be limited to the bottom of the frame. Another example is overhanging foliage at the top of the frame.

A foreground element creates depth. It urges viewers to look beyond the visible and to imagine a deeper scene. Though photographers often link it to landscape photography, they can use the foreground interest technique in any genre. It can also be combined with other compositional techniques.

The foreground interest element can be off-centre. It can provide scale, size, and proportion. It can also create a leading line. You can even use it to incorporate continuance and lead past the main subject... the list goes on and on.

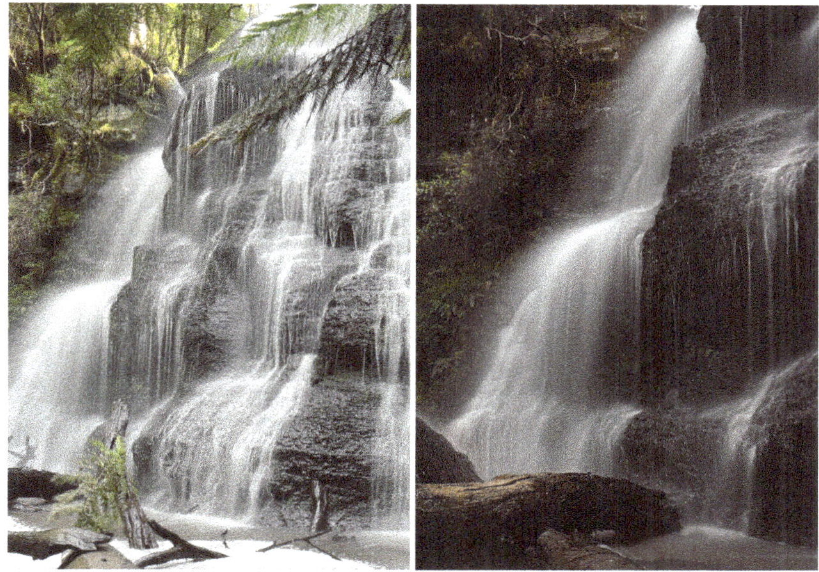

Framing

Framing requires you to utilize different elements and objects to create a 'frame' inside the photo. You could make it out of branches, people, doorways, windows, fences, tunnels, arches, actual picture frames, etc.

As the viewer's attention wanders, framing keeps it from drifting too close to the edge of the photo. It pushes their focus back into the image.

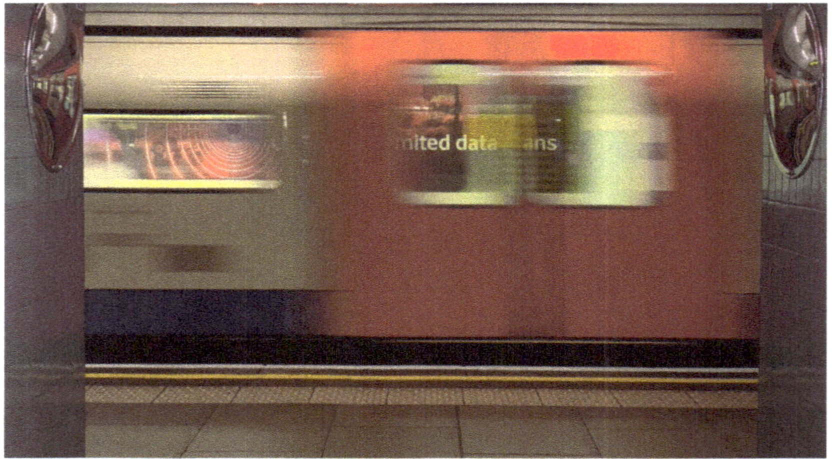

In the photo above, framing is achieved using stationary walls on both sides of the frame and the train's windows!

Rule of odds

This composition technique requires you to include an odd number of either visual elements or groupings. With an even number of elements in a scene, our brains sort them into pairs and compare them, without effort. An odd number of elements, like 3, 5 or 7, allows the viewer's eye to flow around the frame smoothly.

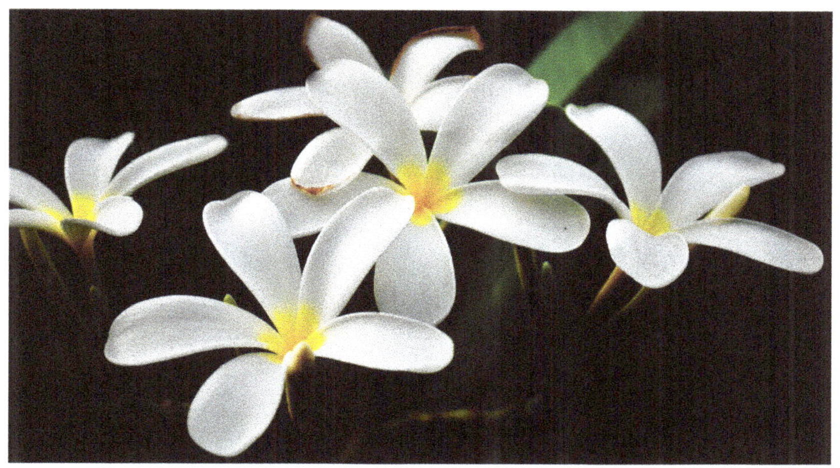

Layering - distance to the camera

You have made it a long way into the book before I can finally share my favourite composition technique. It's layering... closely followed by figure-to-ground and object removal.

Layering is the process of adding dimension and depth to the photo. In scene composition, layering is about positioning elements. It refers to how we place elements in the foreground, middle ground, and background, and how they interact.

As you can see, in the photo below, I have used focus and blur to create layering. The space in front of the subject is slightly out of focus (foreground). The subject is in focus (middle ground). The area behind the subject is out of focus with distance from the camera (background). You can improve the separation of the three layers with changes in color, pattern, or lighting.

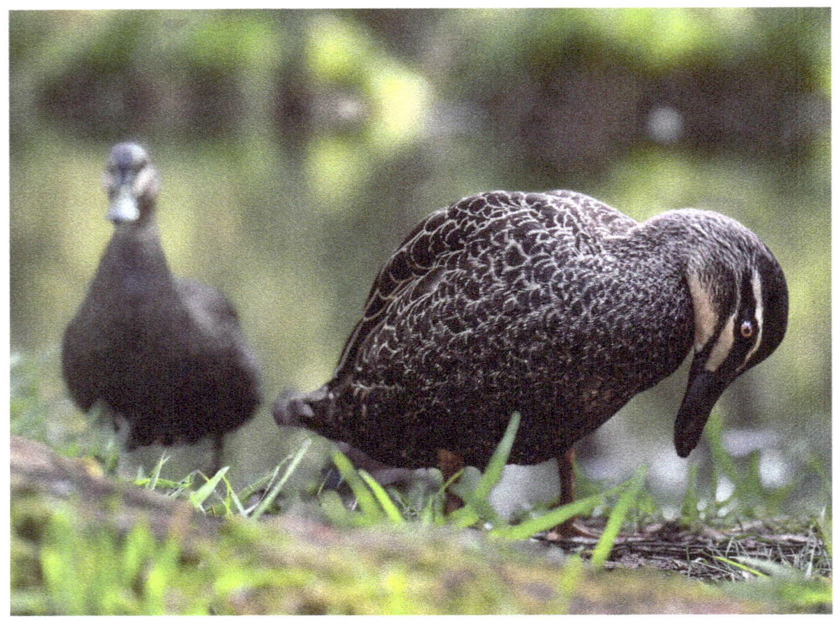

To improve your elements' positioning and make them look natural, you can experiment with depth of field. Do this at capture or during photo editing.

Layering - overlap

Overlapping elements in the photo is another great technique to create depth. It is frequently neglected or executed with low quality. Overlapping elements naturally compel viewers to identify layers in your composition. The differences in the sizes and positions of elements provide visual cues. They help viewers gauge the distance between objects.

Suppose the scene positions all the elements at a distance, causing them to appear small. In this instance, we're forced to rely on diminishing contrast caused by atmospheric conditions (haze, particles in the air). By introducing layering into this scene below, we can create a hierarchy and better manoeuvre the viewers' attention.

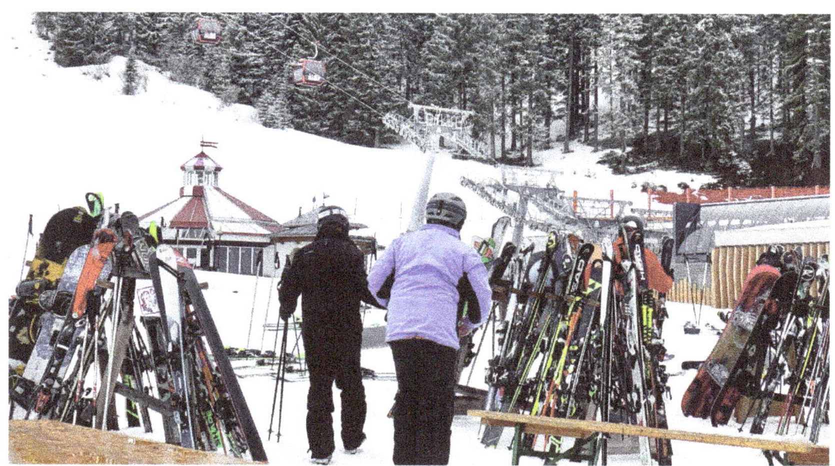

If possible, find a capture angle that aligns the scene's elements. It should also show the distance between objects in the photo.

When using the layering technique, be sure to avoid overlapping elements too much as they can merge and become one giant distraction. This can occur when elements appear to be closely spaced, a similar size, a similar color, or look as if they're entangled rather than overlapping.

Rhythm, time and motion

We've covered several techniques to attract and guide the viewer's attention. They create a 'readable' visual journey or story. This journey also conveys the passage of time as viewers explore the photo.

Some composition techniques are designed to make 'reading' the photo quick and easy for us. Techniques like proximity, common fate, lines, and juxtaposition, help us guide viewers through the photo. Other techniques, like gesture, layering, scale, and shadows, take longer for the viewer to interpret. They must use their imaginations to engage with the mystery they create.

Let's take a moment to go over a simple example and examine the next photo. The repeated elements in the photo are dispersed unevenly, preventing the viewer from easily interpreting the photo from left to right at a consistent pace. Instead, by disrupting that tempo with an interruption, a new rhythm is created that requires more engagement from the viewer. How fascinating is that?

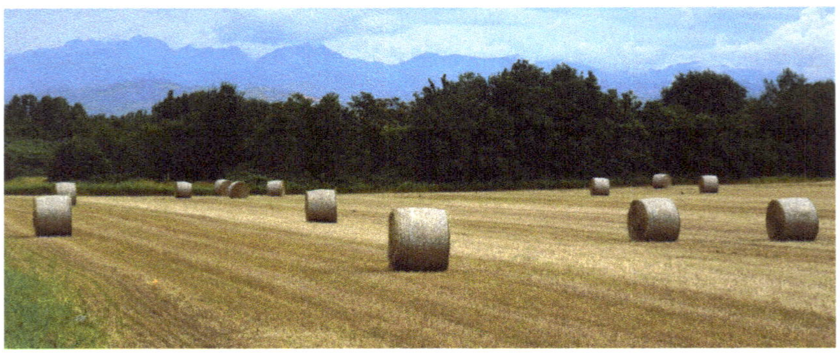

Tip: To slow the viewer's scanning pace, space elements apart. To speed it up, use repetition or space elements closer together.

This technique works better with wide panoramic photos.

Color - monochromatic

Monochromatic color is a fun variation of black and white that uses a single color cast rather than shades of grey. This technique works with photos that contain many lines, shapes, and forms. It's also a great way to reduce distracting colors in your scene and create a greater sense of harmony!

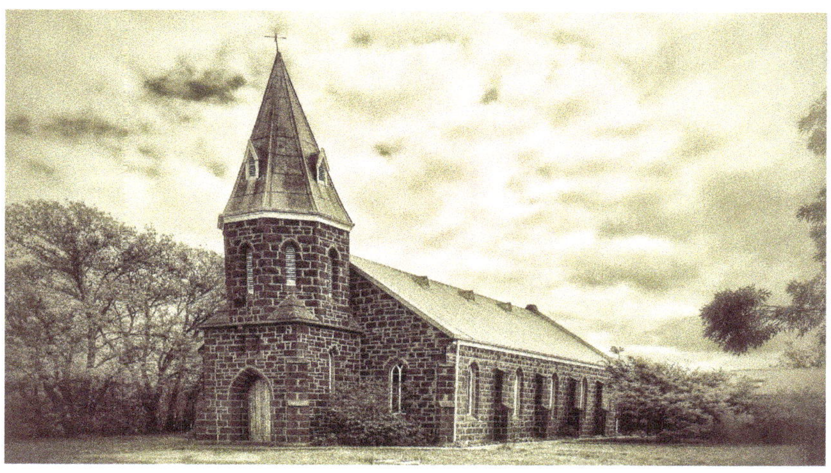

Unlike an artist with a blank canvas, photographers must use what is in front of us. We are often limited to the scene before us. To explore how a single dominant color can affect your photos, try a shooting mode on your camera or the color grading tool in the Lightroom Mobile app.

Color - analogous

As we explore color theory, let's consider the emotions colors evoke. This is key when trying to set a mood in your photography. Colors, and even their absence, relate to emotion. They can enhance the vibe of your photos.

Warm colors usually evoke strong emotions, like happiness and anger. They also suggest hunger, lust, and romance. In contrast, people say that cold colors evoke low-energy feelings. These include tranquillity, sadness, confusion, anxiety, and fear.

Before you can learn to use color in your photography, we must first discuss how color theory categorizes different colors. As we discuss the various methods for classifying color, we will frequently reference the RGB color model, which is also known as the color wheel.

Let's start with adjacent colors on the color wheel, otherwise known as analogous colors in color theory. Analogous color combinations can consist of as few as two colors or as many as half of the colors on the color wheel. This color composition technique works well when we can get close to the subject. It lets us control the included elements and focal points.

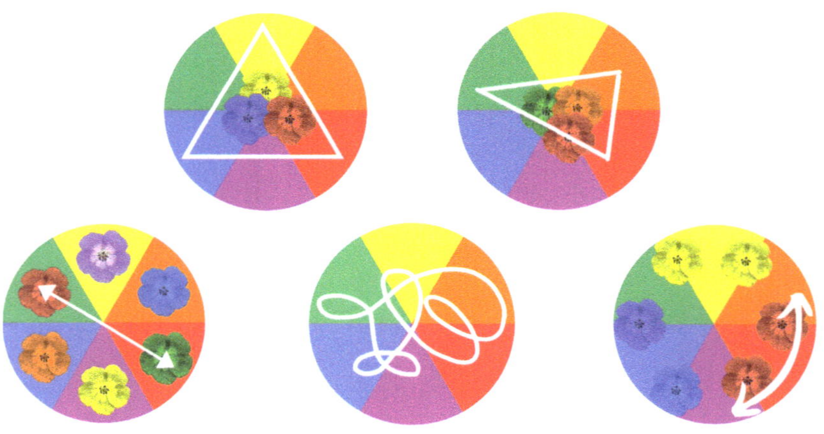

Color contrast - complementary and more

Consider, for a moment, one of your favourite films, television shows, or photographs. Certain scenes and aspects stand out visually in your memory more than others, regardless of their nature. Often, this is because of one compositional element: color contrast.

Contrasting color combos include palettes with: complementary colors, warm colors (reds, oranges, yellows), and cool colors (greens, blues, purples). To see the strong effect of color contrast, look to nature. For example, a red rose with a green leaf. Or, create some with household items, like a bunch of bananas on a purple background.

Use color contrast to juxtapose or isolate elements. This creates a more distinct look and feel in your photos. Classic color contrasts you may want to consider experimenting with are: black and white, orange and blue, yellow and purple, and green and red.

Color contrast - dyadic, triadic and square

Besides using dominant and contrasting colors, limit your color palette. This creates stronger, more impactful photos. Limited color palettes might be dichromatic (2 colors, or dyadic) or trichromatic (3 colors, or triadic). But, they usually include 3 or 4 individual colors at most.

With a limited color palette, use different shades and hues. This can refine or reinforce the harmony or contrast between the colors.

To create a square color palette, imagine that you're drawing a square on the color wheel. Each point of your square lines up with a color, creating a double-split complementary palette.

Be mindful when using square color palettes. This type of composition can cross a line with little difficulty. It may then look more like you avoided a few colors than a technique!

A fantastic tool for identifying what colors are already present in your photo can be found at https://color.adobe.com/create. It's one of the few websites that's better experienced on a mobile than a pc or desktop! You can upload a photo, and it will assess the photo and show you how you went with the color theory.

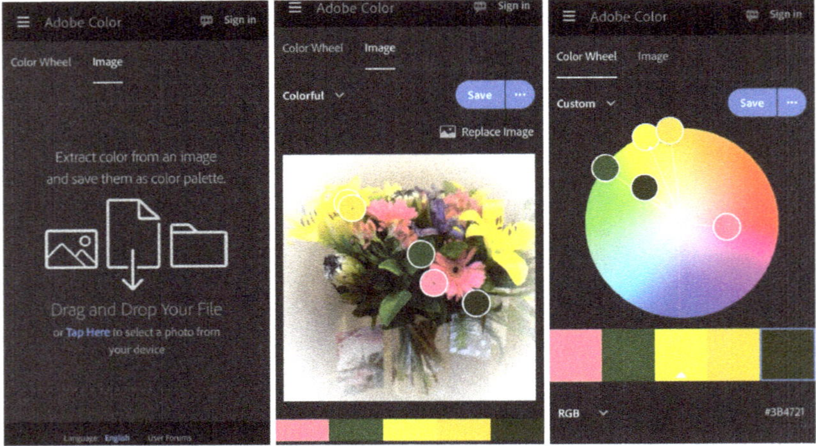

Subject research to improve your photos

Do you find yourself capturing photos of a preferred subject or topic? If so, you can try becoming more familiar with said subject to help you better design the way you capture photos.

If you like taking photos of nature, for example, consider learning about different insects and how they behave. Knowing how bees move around flowers can improve your reactions. It helps you better expect their actions before they happen. This, then, allows you to pre-determine the best angles for capture before you miss the shot.

Garden photography is my favourite example. A cottage garden is a unique style. It uses informal design, diverse plants, and unusual placements. Beneath the random colors and textures is a garden designer. They've carefully planned the landscape and plantings.

From a compositional perspective, gardens have boundaries, a path, and an area of formal entry. A defined entry point serves as a physical and metaphorical gateway. It's a prelude to what lies beyond. An entry is symbolic of a welcome, and as such, can be a great visual anchor to create a starting point for your visual story's narrative. The path from the entry then guides the viewer. It leads through a mass planting of colorful, varied-height plants.

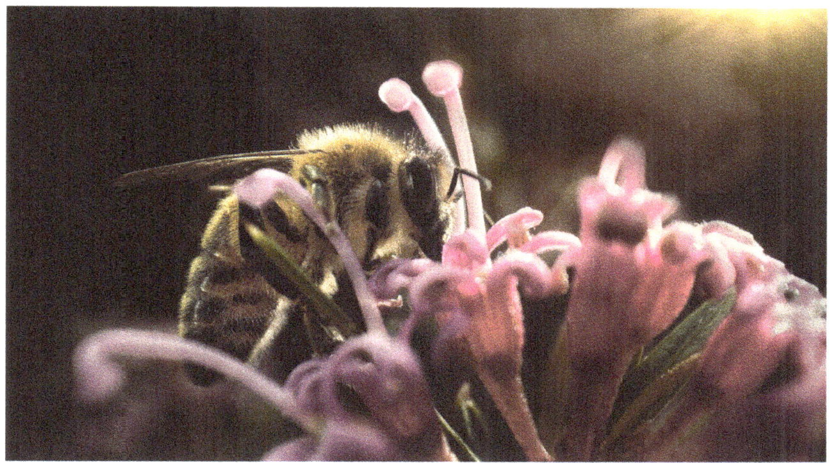

Expanding on the garden design example, let's go over a compositional technique called **'the law of significant enclosure.'** It refers to a space with a sense of refuge that promotes a connection to nature.

We feel enclosed when the vertical edge of the space is at least 1/3 of the length of the horizontal line of the open space. Knowing the law of significant enclosure can enhance your photo's mood or story. You can use it to improve your composition.

Gesture

One of the best secret techniques for capturing a great street photograph is to include gestures and interaction. There is a distinction between the two, so let's cover gesture first.

As a snapshot in time, photos capture the essence of what is happening, as it happened. In photography, gestures can be emphasized or used to support the context of a scene.

We commonly associate a gesture with body position, facial expression, or physical movement. Gestures can also occur in inanimate objects, like a broken wheel on a trolley. The gesture is the suggestion that the trolley is unusable, unstable or imperfect. Also, the gesture refers to a specific, derelict trolley. It is different from the normal, perfect trolley.

Gesture, in a moment, is suggestive. Are you a people watcher? No, I'm not talking about voyeurism! What I mean is, have you ever found yourself looking at someone in public and wondered what their story is? Who they are, what mood they're in, or what do they do for a living? If so, the chances are that you stopped to look because that person gestured something.

Looking for gestures forces you to observe and analyze your surroundings. You must study the details of what is happening around you. Some questions you can use to help you in your gesture analysis are:

- Does the person have something significant about their posture, gait, etc.?
- Do they stand with weight on one or both legs?
- How do they interact with others, if at all?
- What do they do with their hands?
- Do they look people in the eye or look down?

After you answer these questions, you can dig deeper. Consider what each answer implies about the subject of your analysis.

In the photo below, the facial expression on the wall poster of Hugh Laurie is a gesture. He looks like he is questioning, "Why are you taking a photo of the woman on her mobile phone?"

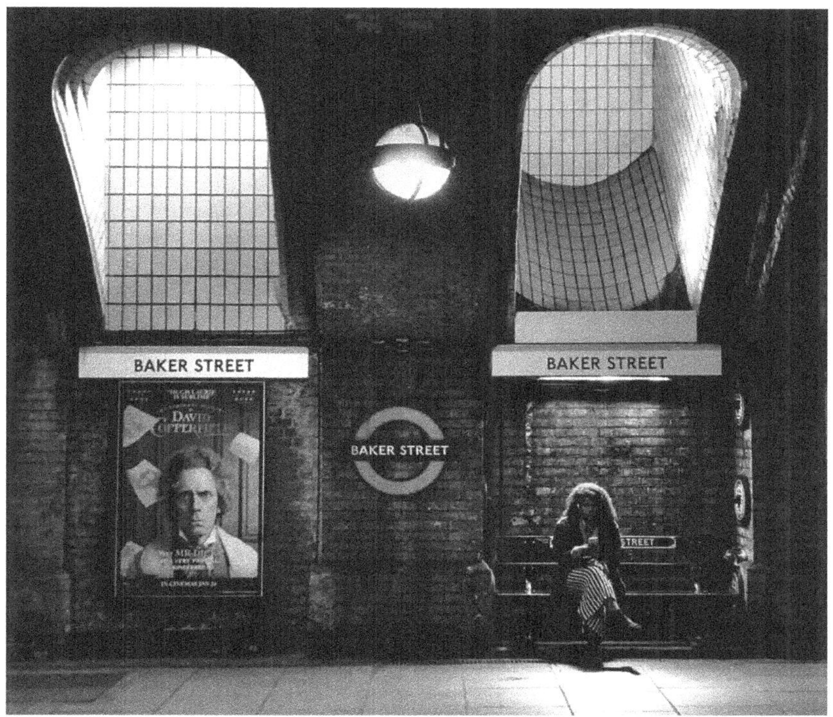

Interaction

One of the main objectives of photo composition is to place different elements in a way that speaks to how they interact and relate to one another. You can use this technique to evoke all viewer reactions and emotions. You may want to create a balanced, harmonious photo. Or, a dramatic, mysterious one with high visual tension.

Another example, and the easiest way to practice, is to capture a person interacting with another person, a pet, or the environment.

I love creative photos of hands because of the inherent interactions and connections they can imply.

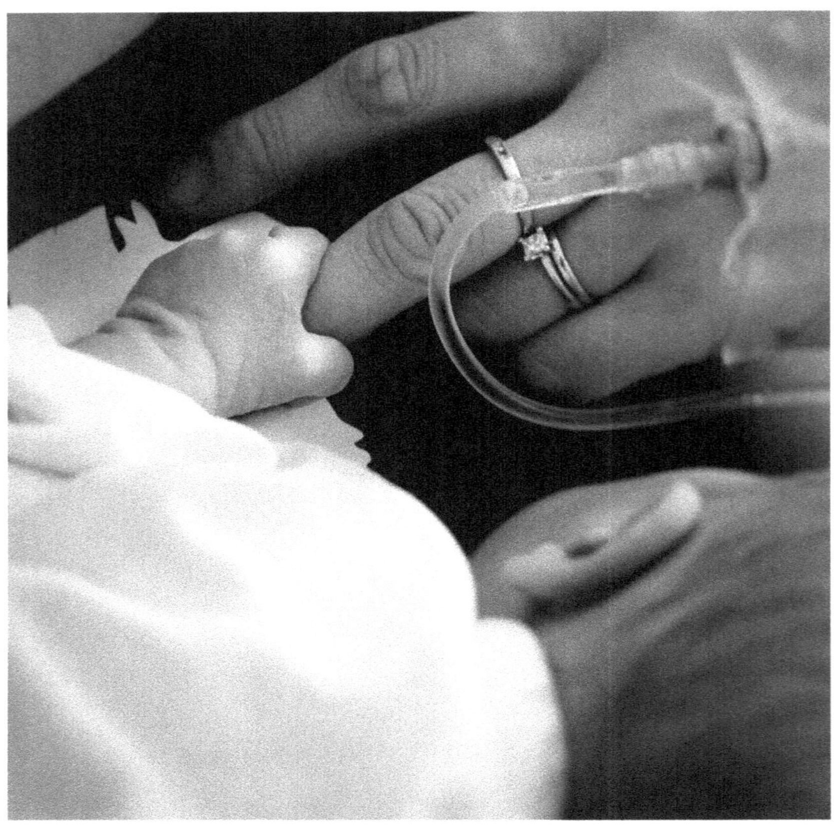

The previous photo is extraordinarily special to me. After our youngest was born, my wife had HELLP Syndrome. It's a pregnancy complication that affects the blood and liver. The medical staff moved her to the ICU. The syndrome put her at risk of having high blood pressure seizures and prevented her from holding our new-born son Riley.

Her biggest fear of not embracing Riley was that the perceived window of initial bond and connection was closing. It was a stressful and emotional time for all of us.

After that experience, this photo of Riley holding my wife's finger became even more special. It shows their interaction.

This relates to composition techniques. It shows that, alone, no element is as powerful as a well-arranged combination of elements. They work together to tell a story and capture a special memory. I edited this photo. I blurred the back of Riley's head. I added a vignette, removed some distractions, and brightened his knuckles to highlight his strong grip.

Tip: Combine interaction with a gesture to create more dynamic, compelling photo compositions.

The decisive moment of action

The decisive moment, for brevity, is a concept by Henri Cartier-Bresson, a French street photographer. He popularised it.

"The photograph itself doesn't interest me. I want only to capture a minute part of reality".

– Henri Cartier-Bresson

This idea isn't a compositional technique. But, it's tied to how you set up and frame your photos. The decisive moment of action requires you to expect and react to a fleeting moment that defines the story.

That sentiment epitomizes the very essence of genuine moments of action. Also, you can greatly improve your photo's meaning. Just combine anticipation, intuition, and preparation for the scene and background.

Some examples of the decisive moment of action at work could be:

- Waiting for a bee to land on a perfectly composed flower

- Finding a unique lighting opportunity in a scene and waiting for pedestrians to walk into it

- Wait near a brightly colored urban area. Then, exploit color combos by finding someone in a complementary or contrasting outfit.

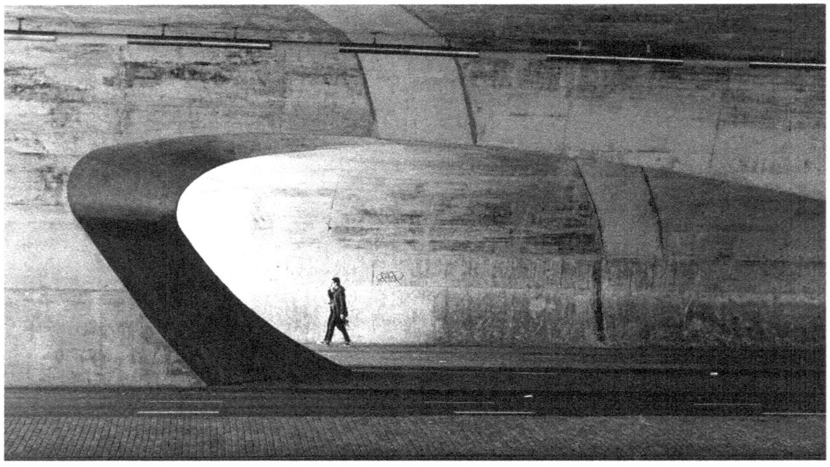

Similar to gesture and interaction, the decisive moment is more about that fleeting and meaningful action shot.

This concept is most used in street photography and people-focused photography. However, a colorful sunrise or dramatic weather event in a landscape photo can also be a decisive moment.

Step 3 - composition techniques

Closure

Figure to ground

Proximity

Common fate

Continuance

Similarity

Minimalism

Scale

Lines - leading

Lines - diagonal

Lines - s-curve and z-curves

Lines - horizontal

Lines - vertical

Line - implied line of sight

Lines - converging lines

Triangles

Golden ratio

Phi grid

Golden spiral

Fibonacci spiral

Baroque diagonal

Focal points - hierarchy

Foreground interest

Framing

Rule of odds

Layering - distance

Layering - overlap

Rhythm, time and motion

Colour - monochromatic

Colour - harmonious

Colour - contrast

Colour contrast - advanced

Subject research

Gesture

Interaction

The decisive moment of action

STEP 4: Enhance Composition - Mobile Editing Tools

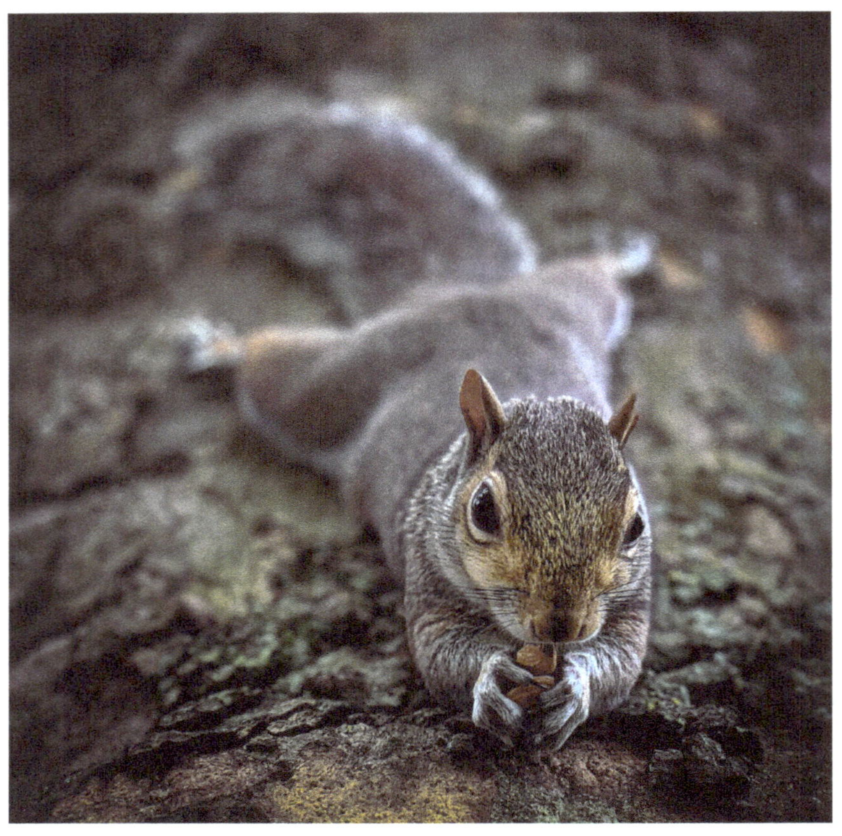

You can use Step 4 to refine your photography and better direct the viewer's attention with editing tools. This is the fun part of photography. When done right, it is the final touch that makes your photo stand out. It elevates it to a WOW photo that viewers will appreciate.

This is the most powerful step in composition. You can enhance your composition efforts, enhancing the visual flow through the photo. Editing can create balance, add visual tension, and even change the visual hierarchy of elements. Here, you can be creative. You can even make many versions of the same photo using global (whole photo) and local (area-specific) adjustments.

I am quite aware that the interface or steps in the tools described in this next section can change in future app updates. I have deliberately avoided app screen captures and attempted to keep the descriptions rather general.

Next, we will explore several free or low-cost mobile photo editing apps. They are in Google Play and the App Store: Snapseed, Adobe Lightroom, PicsArt, After Focus, TouchRetouch, and Handy Photo.

Most of the compositional tools covered in this step are designed to complement your existing editing process. Considering these techniques during capture can reduce your editing later.

For example, if you remove a bottle of water from the desk or move a branch behind the flower before you take the photo, you won't have to remove it in editing.

During Steps 1 - 3, we primarily concentrated on how to think about and craft a photo throughout the capturing process. In Step 4, we'll focus on the editing tools available to us to *further direct the viewer's attention and enhance their visual experience.* And, as with the previous three steps, there is some crossover of techniques.

Visual tension - further enhance

The position of your subject and the amount of space around it can create a significant impact on the aesthetics and feel of your photos. You can introduce visual tension in your photography by cropping the subject close to the edge of the frame to grab viewers' attention.

Visual tension can also have a negative effect. Positioning your subject in close contact with the edge can leave viewers wondering, "What would it look like with more space?" or, "What is beyond the edge of the photo?".

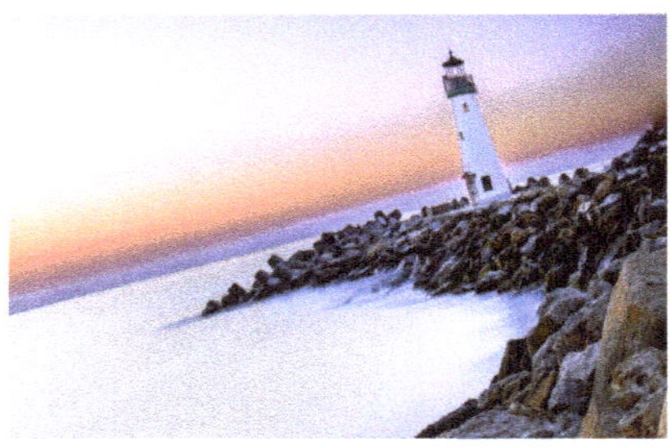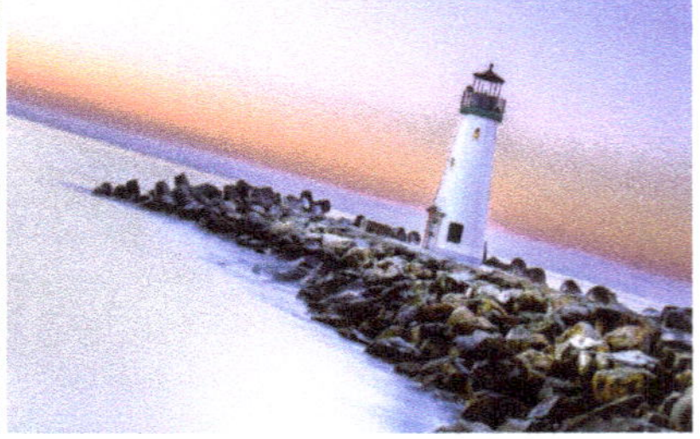

To create mystery and intrigue, use visual tension in your picture. It will urge viewers to use their imagination. But, in a calmer, more relaxing photo (like a seascape), it can have a more negative impact.

Straighten - using the Snapseed perspective tool

If you're already inside our online community, then you already know that I have an issue with crooked photos! Unless a photo is tilted for artistic effect, it must be straight and level.

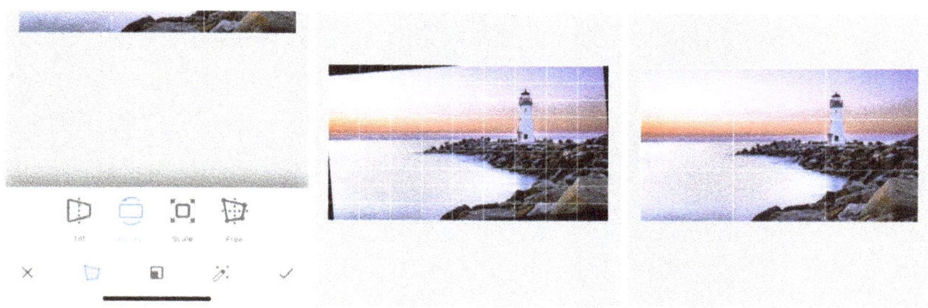

Instead of just using the Rotate tool in your phone's camera editor, check the Perspective tool in the Snapseed app. Most rotate and straighten tools skew or crop corners. But, the rotate option in Snapseed's Perspective tool is a great alternative.

The Snapseed perspective tool lets you add canvas to your photos. It fills in the blanks using your original photo as a reference. It does this without cropping, distorting, or skewing the photo.

Cropping - #1 tool to re-compose - Snapseed

Cropping is one of the most powerful techniques you can use to create compositional opportunities. The crop tool has a practical use. It lets you zoom into a photo and change the aspect ratio for different printing or posting options. Most importantly, cropping helps to recompose a photo. It better conveys our intention, story, and creativity.

Aspects - Aspect ratios

Cropping to different aspects, or aspect ratios, allows you to optimize photos for different outputs. My aspect ratio preference is 16:9 in landscape orientation. This works for my online tutorials and displays on the TV at home.

Cropping photos to a square aspect ratio of 1:1 creates an ideal size for posting on social media. You can adjust your photo size to match the frames and displays. This depends on how you will display them and if you will print them.

Remove distractions

You can remove distracting subjects and speckles of bright light from the edges by cropping your photos a little tighter (closer).

Isolating the subject

Cut out sections of the photo to isolate the subject from a distracting background. A more prominent subject helps to communicate your message clearly and makes it easier to interpret in the photo.

Symmetry and balance

You can also use the crop tool to reposition subjects. This improves balance and makes the photo more pleasing.

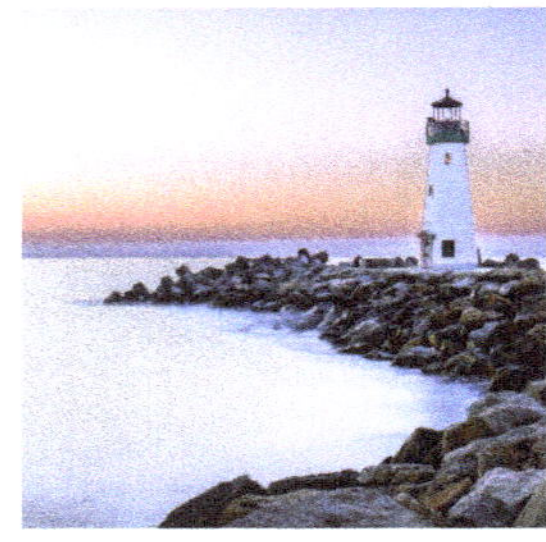 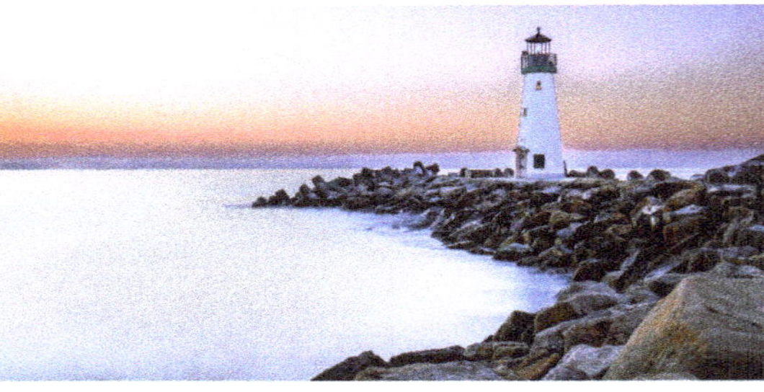

People

Cropping in closer can elevate the viewers' feelings of intimacy and familiarity with the subject. In portrait photography, for example, cropping can bring the subjects' eyes closer to the camera. This enables a connection with the viewer. If your photos have awkward hand or leg positions, use the crop tool. You can remove the offending limb or, if you prefer, the whole person.

Ruthless crop

You've likely heard photographers suggest ignoring composition and design rules. If you've read this far, you know how vital it is to understand and appreciate different techniques and tools. Without some knowledge of composition, it's hard to complement the photo's intent and achieve the desired outcome.

An example of moving away from traditional compositional techniques is an awkward or seemingly random crop.

The results may create new visual tension or a sense of mystery. This happens when the expected visual cues are absent or presented unexpectedly. The worst that could happen is you don't like the new photo. In that case, you can just revert the changes to return it to its original state.

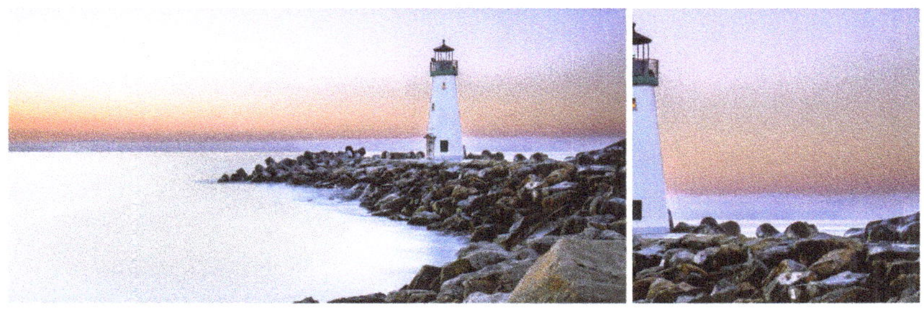

Frame edges – border patrol!

I like to do a 'border patrol' of sorts, looking around the edges to ensure no bright spots or other elements compete for the viewers' attention.

These distractions act like magnets for our attention. They pull us away from the main subject and the photo's narrative.

When our attention moves to the edge and out of the photo, it requires mental load and motivation for us to return that attention to the photo. I know it sounds silly. But trust me. In the online world, these little things matter! They can make a big difference in attracting and keeping viewers' attention.

Cropping is a great way to remove something on the edges that diminishes the viewer's focus and understanding of the subject. Be mindful, though, that awkwardly cut-off elements can create unwanted visual tension.

Perspective editing - perspective and liquify tool

The Perspective tool in the Snapseed app corrects lens distortion. It also helps enhance details for better aesthetics.

Next, let's cover each of the options inside the Snapseed Perspective tool.

Tilt

After you tap on Tilt, swipe up and down, or left and right. Swiping up and down changes the view. It looks like the camera angle changed. In real estate photography, this alters the angle of the walls. It makes the bottom appear either more stretched or narrower.

Changing the horizontal perspective alters the capture angle. It makes it look like you captured the photo further left or right than you did. Alter this too much, though, and it quickly stretches the photo, giving it an unrealistic appearance.

Rotate

The standalone Rotate option within Tools will rotate, zoom in, and crop the edges of your photos. The Rotate option within Perspective will also rotate the photo. However, it will not zoom in. Instead, it adds to the original photo and fills in the blank spaces with content from surrounding areas. This is especially helpful if you have a subject positioned close to the edges and you're unable to crop when straightening.

Scale

This is a great option to effectively 'squash' your photo either vertically or horizontally. You may be thinking, "Why would I want to do that?" Well, once you start playing with this option, you will start to see how it can be used.

I occasionally use the Scale tool for landscape photos to compress the middle of the photo and make it appear more like a panoramic photo. The Scale tool also allows us to avoid cropping and risk compromising or removing the foreground and/or the sky.

Before I use the scale tool on a photo, I will change the fill mode to black more often than not. Then, I crop out the black section to keep the new "squashed" version.

Free

The Freeform function is a lot of fun, but it can quickly get out of control. This is a feature that you just have to spend some time playing with and experimenting.

Start by long-pressing a corner and dragging it out and away from the photo to stretch the photo. The rest of the photo will stretch with it and keep most of its shape. You can also hold and drag the middle of the top, bottom, or either side edge to stretch two corners at once.

As you can see, this is quite a powerful feature of Snapseed. Sometimes, depending on the content near the edges, the Smart Mode produces a less-than-ideal result. If this occurs, you can either crop out the unwanted section or use the Healing tool (covered below in Simplicity - removing items) to repair the area.

Liquify

A step up from the Freeform tool inside Snapseed, the liquify tool is another tool that's a blast to play around with. My preferred liquify tool is on the PicsArt app and can be located inside Tools > Stretch > Warp.

Photos of shorelines or other outdoor areas with no references benefit most from using the liquify tool. If you start bending the edges of buildings with the liquify tool, you'll find that it starts to look funky very quickly.

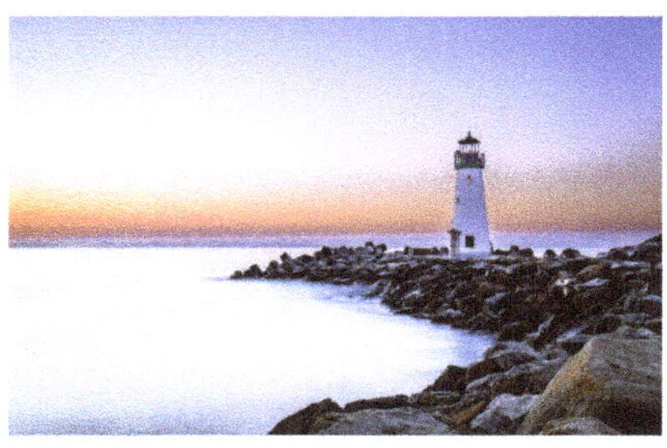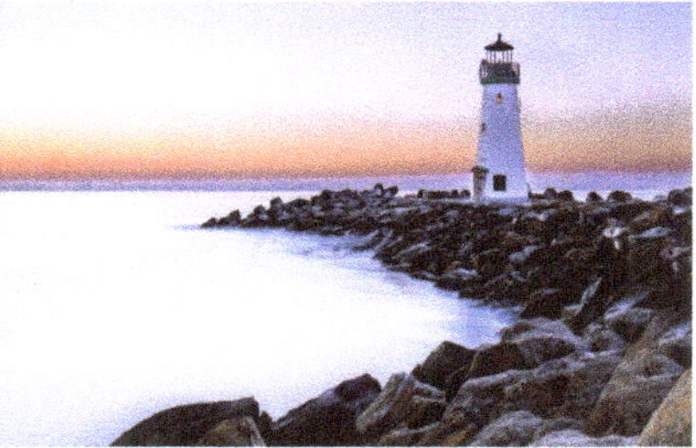

Add extra canvas - Expand tool

After taking a photo, we sometimes wish it were horizontal instead of vertical. Or, we want to extend the sides for a panoramic shot.

The Expand tool in the Snapseed app adds canvas space to your photo. It won't affect the quality or resolution.

The Expand tool inside Snapseed allows you to drag out the edge of your photo without stretching it. Instead, it fills the extra space created with the Smart fill mode, solid white or solid black.

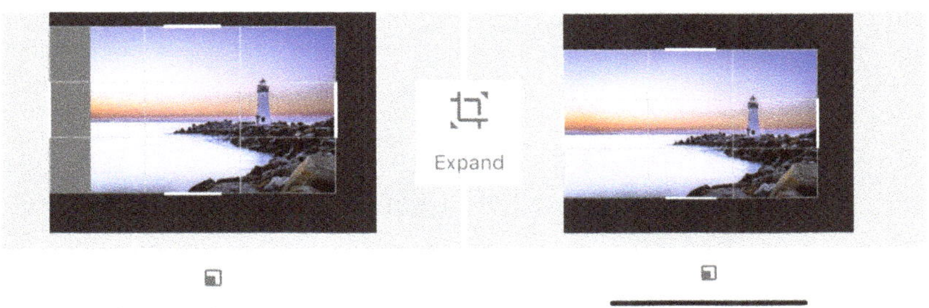

Expanding one edge of the frame allows you to place the main subject further off-centre in the frame.

Selective sharpness - Blur tool - Snapseed

As a viewer, our eye is inherently attracted to the in-focus areas of a photo. Blurring the areas around the main focus steers the viewer's attention back to the sharp parts of the photo.

The Lens Blur tool inside Snapseed is super easy to use. Tap on Tools then Lens Blur. By default, two circles appear on the screen. The inner circle is the area that is in focus. The area between the second outer circle and the edges of the frame is blurred. The space between the two circles is the transition between in-focus and out-of-focus areas.

Place your finger on the blue dot and drag it onto the subject that you want in focus. Next, pinch and zoom your fingers vertically and then horizontally to increase/decrease the size of the area in focus.

You can then adjust both the strength of the blur and the transition distance between the in-focus and blurred areas.

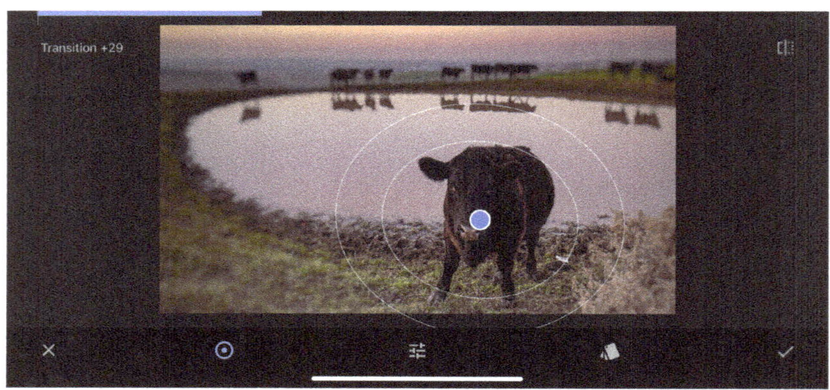

Linear blur - After Focus

Blurring the background creates depth. It also reduces distractions from clutter. You can use the linear option inside the Snapseed Blur tool. However, the blur transition from one edge to the opposite edge will also blur any foreground interest. I use an app called After from developer MotionOne.

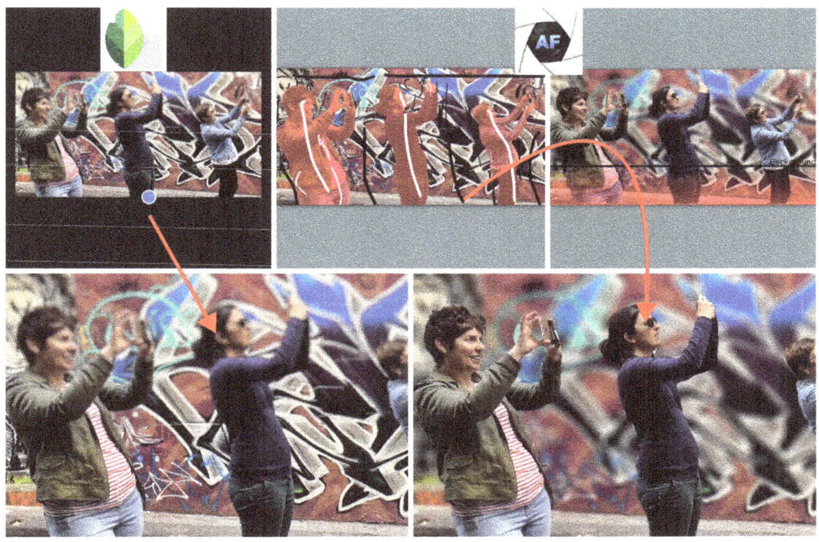

This app lets you choose which part of a photo to focus on. It will slightly blur some areas and blur the background to the selected strength. A mask overlay displays to display your selections.

The next step to make the linear blur look more realistic is the faded background feature. This option allows you to gradually fade the blur effect from the bottom edge to the top edge avoiding the elements you selected to be unaffected. I use this all the time to add depth to my compositions.

Gradation - smooth edit transition - Lightroom mobile

Similar to linear focus, gradation refers to a smooth, gradual transition from 0 - 100% of an edit adjustment. You may know some examples of gradation. They are the transitions from dark to light, small to large. They are also analogous colours, directions, shapes, brightness values, intensity, temperature, and textures.

The easiest way to add a gradation is the Mask tool inside Adobe Lightroom mobile app - requiring a subscription account. We will cover masks in more detail later. Let's quickly explore the Linear mask to create a gradation.

After adding a linear gradient mask, you can change the mask overlay color. You can also change the original photo's color. This will show you where your adjustment will affect the photo and how much the mask is blended.

If you are already familiar with Lightroom mobile, you can next apply adjustments in the Light, Color, Effects and Color panels. It's perfect to blend towards a darkened, muted edge of the frame to enhance the composition and bring attention back to the photo.

Tip: You can apply more than one linear mask in a photo if you would like many gradations.

Shadows and highlights - Snapseed

Quick reminder that shadows are the darker parts of the photo and highlights are the brighter area of the photo.

In photography, the dynamic range is the range of luminance. It is the difference between the darkest and brightest tones that the camera can capture. Cameras measure this range in increments called stops. Most of us have cameras with a sensor that captures 14 stops. Some of us have a smartphone or a dedicated camera. They use software to extend the dynamic range. They automatically brighten shadows and darken highlights. This produces a photo closer to what our eyes see (24 stops of luminance).

Why am I sharing this in a composition book?

To direct the viewer's attention to the colors and textures in the clouds, then reduce the highlights. To reveal the details and structures in shadows, increase (boost) the shadows.

Shadows - crushing the blacks - Lightroom mobile

Most photographers boost shadows to create a more aesthetic photo, closer to what the human eye sees. My preference is to do the opposite! I like to add mystery to the shadows.

When we darken the shadows, they become blocks of black nothing, eventually voiding details and increasing the mystery. The process is called crushing the blacks. Until now, we've discussed how our eye is drawn to bright things. But, you can also use solid black areas to forge a sense of dominance that is equally compelling and captures viewer attention.

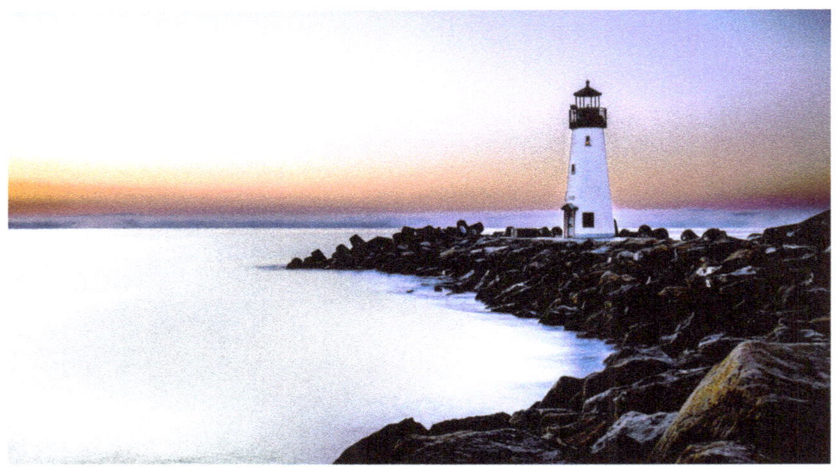

You can crush the blacks by decreasing the shadows inside the Tune Image tool in Snapseed. My preference is to use the Blacks slider inside the Light panel of Lightroom mobile app.

Local adjustments - Brush tool - Snapseed

This is where you start to take your photos to the next stage. Every photo has parts of the photo that need adjustment independent of the rest of the photo.

A big advantage of editing apps over your phone's built-in tools is the ability to selectively edit your photo, exactly where you want.

The Brush tool lets you swipe your finger over the photo. It adjusts: Dodge & Burn (a light brightness tweak), Exposure (a stronger one), Temperature (adds a blue or orange tint), and Saturation (makes colors more vibrant)..

You can use the standard pinch and zoom gesture to get in closer and apply more precise local adjustments.

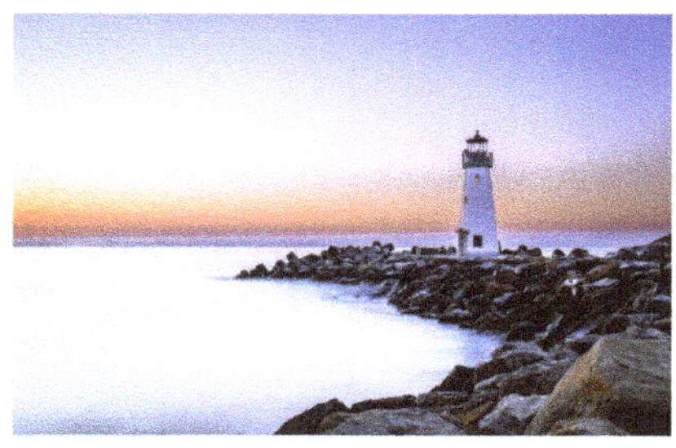 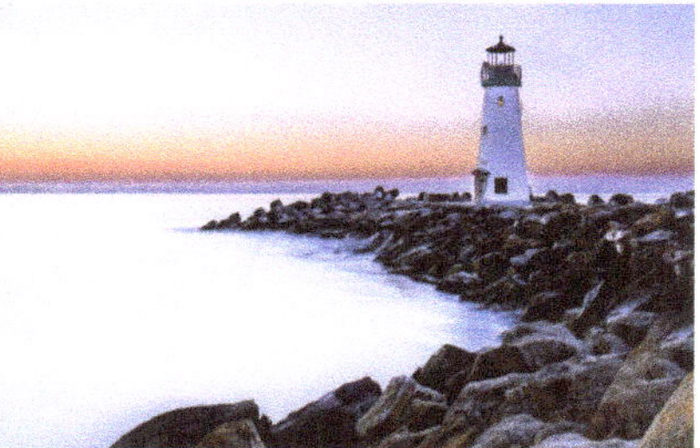

Tip: The Brush tool allows you to perform dodge and burn editing and adjust exposure, temperature and saturation.

Local adjustments - Selective tool - Snapseed

The brush tool is great for quick fixes to saturate some colours or darken backgrounds or brighten someone's face. The selective tool, yet, provides a much more accurate selection.

The process involves dropping a pin on the photo. Then, use the pinch and zoom gesture to adjust a selection of similar surrounding tone/color pixels (tiny dots on the photo). You can then select to increase/decrease brightness, contrast, saturation or structure (sharpening).

As you can imagine, this tool is very powerful to brighten/darken, sharpen/blur, saturate and mute colours anywhere in the photo. It is one of the best tools for enhancing or even changing the visual hierarchy of elements in the photo.

Tip: The Selective tool adjusts brightness, contrast, saturation and structure (aggressive sharpening).

Masking - Snapseed

The Brush and Selective tools are great. However, there are some tools within Snapseed that you cannot apply locally as an area-specific adjustment.

What is masking?

When you make an adjustment, the new version of the image is stacked on top of the previous version, hiding the previous layer. Masking is the process of selectively revealing and/or hiding parts or all of the previous layer.

How it works in Snapseed

Each time you make an adjustment inside Snapseed, it automatically saves a new version over top, referred to as stacking. In other apps, this is known as layers. You can go back to these layers to refine the adjustment or select exactly where to apply them in the photo. The masking tool works the same way as the brush tool requiring you to swipe with your finger. You can refine the edges by pinching and zooming to get closer. You can adjust the opacity of the mask (revelation of the adjustment) in percentages of 25, 50, 75 and 100%.

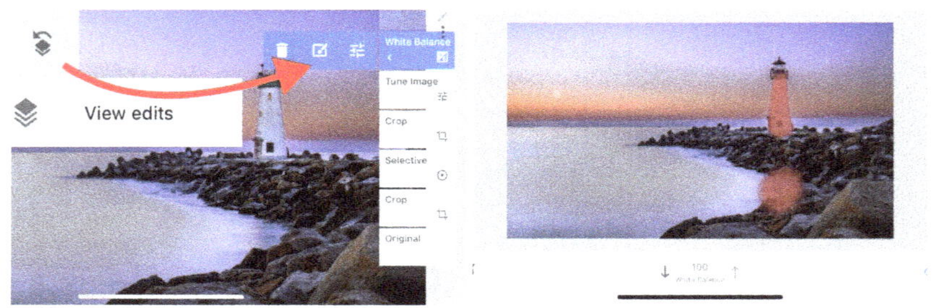

Masking - Lightroom mobile

Masking (previously called Selections) is a paid subscription tool.

After you tap on the Masking icon, tap on the + icon. You have a full suite of options now; subject, sky, brush, linear gradient, radial gradient, color range and luminance range. On the iPhone, if you capture a Portrait mode photo, you also have a depth range to make a selection of elements within a certain distance of the iPhone lens.

An app upgrade in late 2021 added a 'game-changing' ability. I could add and subtract multiple selections to refine a search. It was a game-changer for me.

When you tap on either sky or subject, machine learning will analyse your photo and look for tell-tale signs of what the sky or main subject should be. The sky will look for typical colours and tones and make a selection from the top edge of the frame toward the centre. It is surprisingly accurate!

Looking at the blue sky outside, you will notice that the sky transitions from dark blue to light blue on the horizon. You can now select the sky and subtract a linear mask. This will gradually reduce your adjustment toward the horizon for a more natural result.

Linear mask - this is ideal for darkening toward the edges of the frame to bring attention back to the photo.

Radial mask - this is ideal for local areas that you want to brighten. You can even invert your selection. We will cover that in more detail later in the vignette.

Color and luminance range. These two tools are great for refining a selection to a specific tone or color. This is very handy to darken or mute areas of the photo in a more natural-looking way than a brush tool.

Selective colour - Lightroom mobile

Sticking to techniques and tools for attracting viewer attention, let's talk about selective colour. A highly effective tool, you can use selective colour to exaggerate colour in your photography. You can also mute all colours, except those of the visual elements that you want the viewer to notice.

My preference for this type of edit is the Colour Mix inside Lightroom mobile app. Tap on Colour then Mix to bring up the eight colour channel. Reduce the saturation of each colour to create a grayscale photo. This tool uses the original colour information in the photo. To restore individual colors, adjust the colour channel saturation sliders.

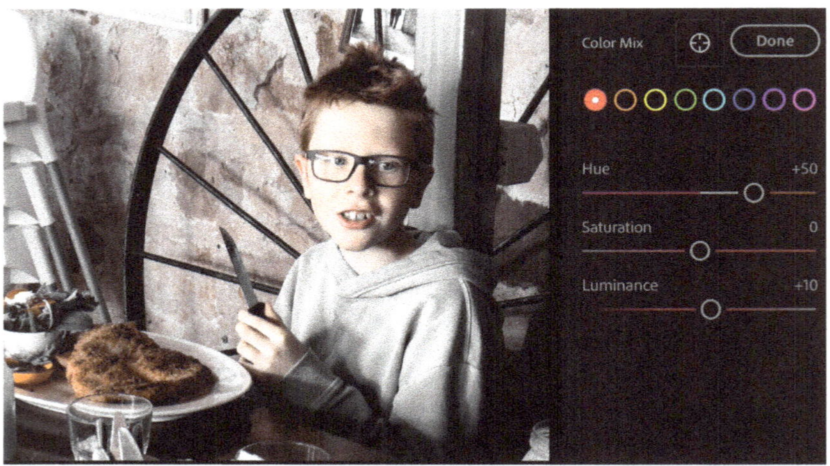

Vignette

A vignette is a soft border overlay. It darkens or brightens the photo's edges. This pulls the viewer's attention to the centre of the frame.

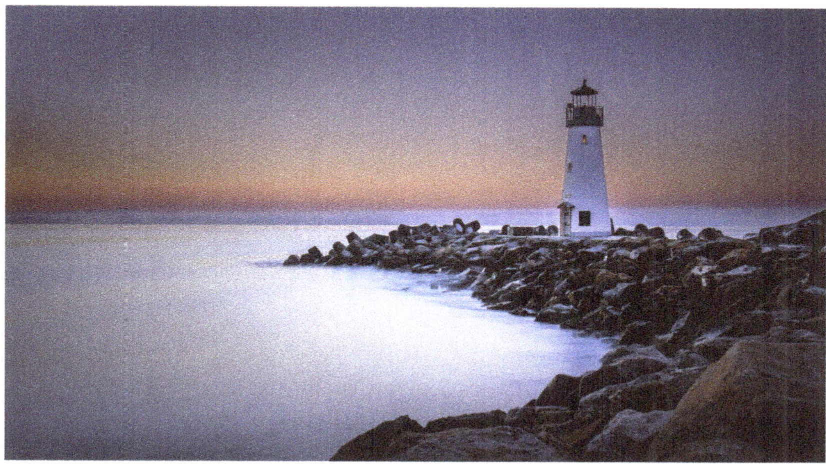

My preferred mobile editing app for adding a vignette is Lightroom mobile. There are two methods; the vignette inside the Effect panel or using an inverted radial mask (subscription needed). My method using the Vignette tool involves swiping all the way to the left on the Vignette slider to see the full strength of the effect. Then, adjust the midpoint, feather, roundness, and highlights. After that, reduce the vignette to the desired amount. The other option is to add a mask, select the radial mask, and tap and stretch over the area you would like to be inside the vignette. Invert the mask and then make adjustments inside the Light and Effects panel.

Add light flares and sunbursts using PicsArt

Who doesn't love the warm glow of the morning sun? Even if you're not a morning person, we all know that bliss when the afternoon sun hits our skin after a great day. And it can also be replicated in your photography using sunbursts and light flares.

Tip: Adding a sunflare or sunburst to a photo can add to its overall mood, tone, and narrative.

When you add any type of lighting element, remember to be mindful of where and how you position it relative to other elements in the frame. The photo's elements can cast shadows and distort highlights. They clearly indicate the direction of your light source. If you place a sunburst on the opposite side of the existing direction of light in the photo, it will look unbalanced and fake!

PicsArt (iOS and Android - free) - Open the photo and swipe left across the tool icons to reveal Lens Flare. Tap on the desired lens flare, then use the tools to rotate, move, re-orientate, and change the hue (color) and opacity.

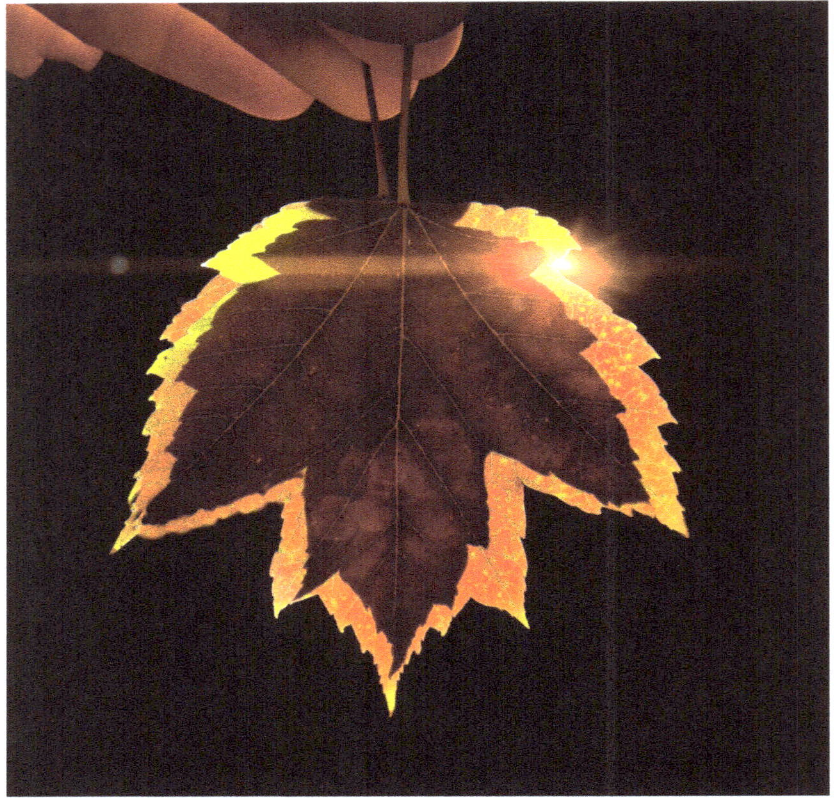

Removing distracting elements - TouchRetouch app

You know you have experienced this... a photo with an object sticking out of someone's head or a distracting element that you wish you could just get rid of.

A photographer's goal is to break a scene into its parts. They must find a visual anchor and a good position. Then, they must use the existing elements to create a flow. This should tell a story that supports their intent.

Removing distracting elements to create a simple and 'clean' photo is the real magic!

Another way you can think about this is to ask yourself questions to determine whether an element is vital to a scene. Some questions you may want to consider are:

- Does the element change the story or context of the scene?
- Is the element necessary to communicate the photo's intent or narrative?
- How does the element change how other elements are perceived, if at all?
- Does removing the element change how the viewer 'reads' the photo?

You can do a quick object removal inside Snapseed using the Healing tool. My favorite app for basic to very advanced object removal is TouchRetouch by developer AdvaSoft. The Healing tool in Snapseed is limited. It analyzes the pixels around where you swipe on the photo. It then tries to use that to fill in the area with new pixels.

TouchRetouch has an object, line, mesh removal tool and a clone stamp. The cloning tool allows you to choose the reference point you want to copy manually and lets you determine the effect's opacity. You can even restore the original photo underneath the replaced area to refine the clone and blend it in naturally. After a bit of a learning curve, this app will be an integral part of your photo editing process.

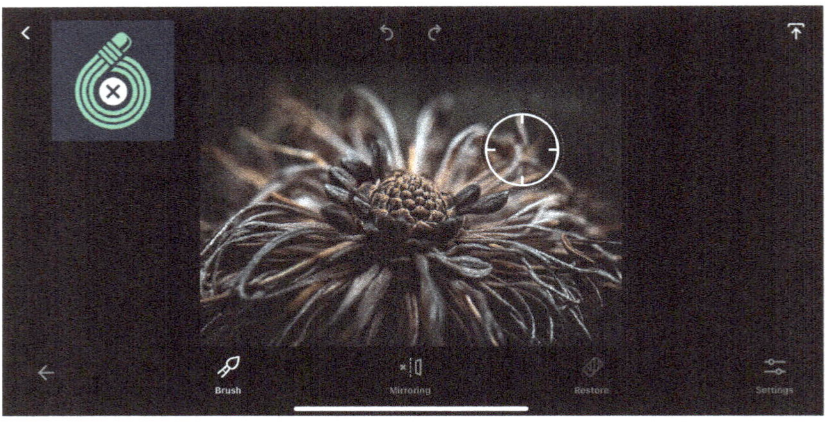

Reposition elements - Handy Photo app

Finally, it's the last one! You've made it to the end! And, luckily, I've saved one of the best tools for last.

Sometimes, we don't have the luxury of access or time to reposition elements in the scene. However, with a little bit of editing, you can remove items... and reposition them!

My favourite app for doing this is a $2.49 app: Handy Photo by developer AdvaSoft. But this app can do so much more than just move objects. And it's the best I've found available on both Google Play and the App Store, at least so far!

Here's how you can use the Handy Photo app to reposition or remove elements in your photos:

Open a photo > tap on the hand icon to expand the menu > move me > select the brush or lasso to make your selection.

You can pinch your fingers on the screen to zoom in on the photo and use the eraser tool to make a more precise selection. Next, tap on the icon that contains an outline of a tree. Click on the arrow and silhouette of a tree, and drag it to the new location. Then, tap on the icon containing two tiles and the down arrow. Tap on the icon that features two tiles and two arrows.

Note: This app may update its user interface, and the instructions may vary from the actual process.

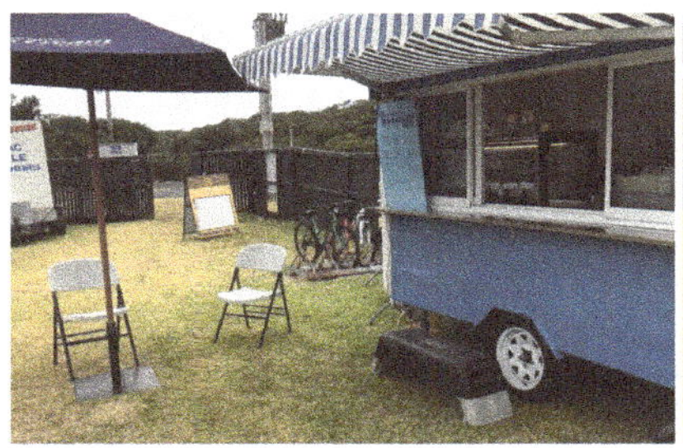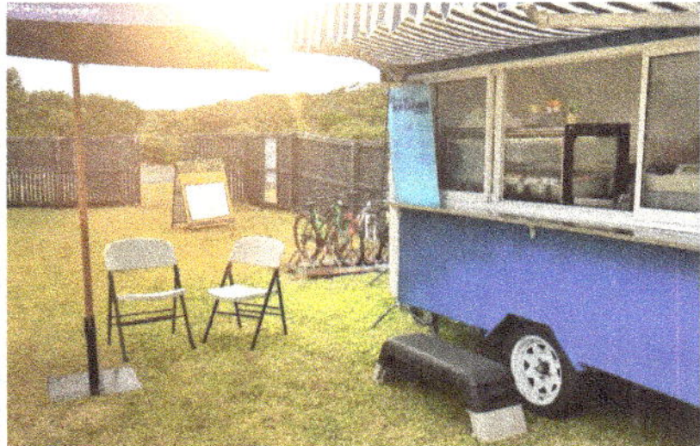

Step 4 - composition tools using various apps

Visual tension
Straighten
Cropping
Perspective
Expand tool
Selective sharpness
Linear sharpness
Gradation
Shadows/highlights
Shadows - Crush the blacks

Local adjustments
Selective tool
Masking
Masking
Selective colour
Vignette
Light flares
Removing distraction
Reposition elements

Practice Activities

Activity 1 - Take the same photo in nine ways

This first activity encourages you to experiment with angles and distances. Find the details that make a subject or location unique.

The subject can be anything- a toy car, a bowl of fruit on a table, a flower outside in the garden. When taking photos, shoot from all angles and distances. Use front, rear, side, low, and high angles. You can also use props or shoot at different times of day for photos with different lighting.

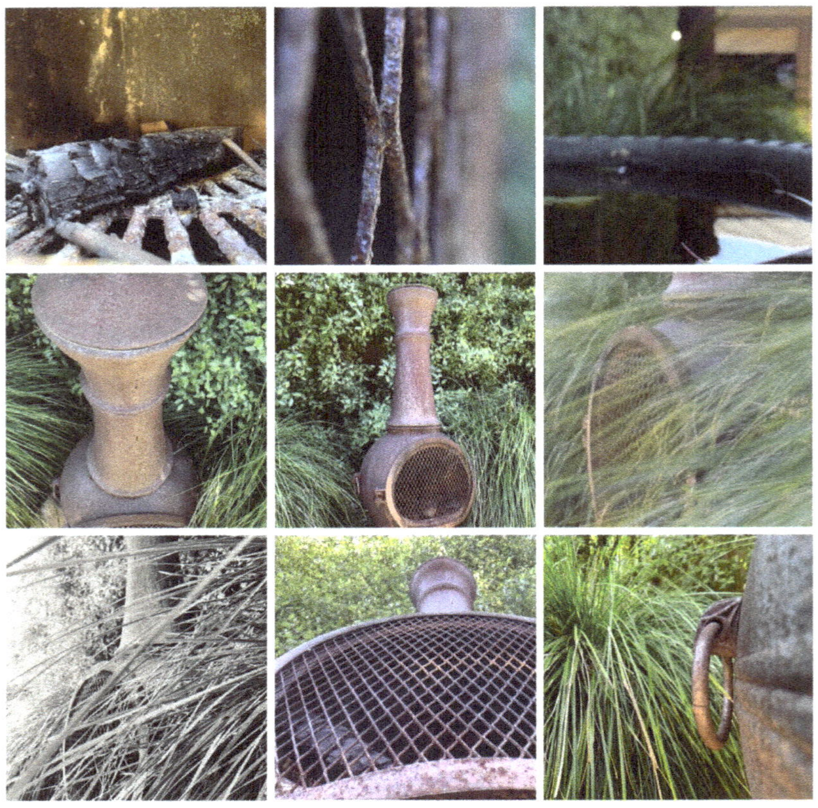

Activity 2 - Change the visual hierarchy

Find one of your favorite photos. Then, see if you can identify which elements of the scene grab your attention first, second, and so on. Are there any distinct colors, tones, lines, textures, or shapes that guide your attention from one focal point to another?

To enhance the picture, try editing the perspective, colors, tones, lines, or textures in a photo editing app. Use the compositional editing tools from Step 4 of the system. You can even re-crop the photo to make the visual journey more compelling, as I did in the examples below.

Want to challenge yourself? You can also attempt to change the hierarchy order to redirect the viewer's attention in an entirely new and different way from the original photo.

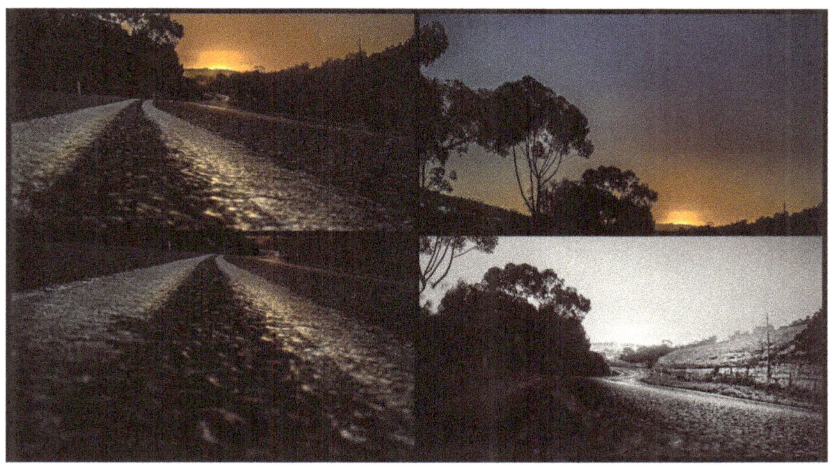

Activity 3 - Breakdown a favorite photo

This activity is the key to unlocking the ultimate transformation through this system. As photo enthusiasts, we often struggle to explain what makes a photo appeal to us.

Pick out a favorite photo and take a few minutes to try and overcome this challenge. As you do so, please check the section containing the full list of techniques and tools toward the end of this book. You can tick them off as you find them.

50 techniques and tools in a single photo!

As adults, we all learn differently. You may prefer to learn the four-step system. Then, apply it to your existing knowledge of composition techniques. You may prefer a comprehensive resource that you can skim-read. If you prefer to learn through video, then the below video walks you through all the techniques and tools I identified from this book.

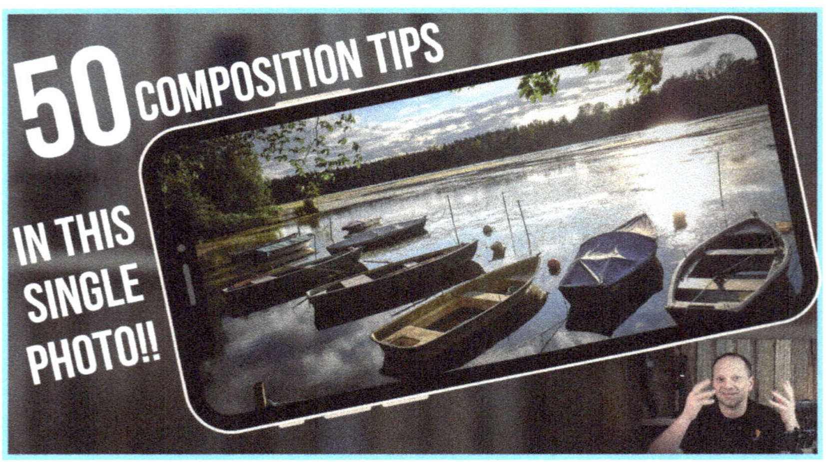

View the video at bit.ly/50composition

In the above video, you can identify all these composition techniques and tools...

Step 1: Prepare and position the camera

- Camera height - squeeze/expand the background
- Asymmetrical balance
- Lighting - direction, strength, and quality
- Shadows, side lighting and textures - affect depth
- Reflections
- Atmospheric perspective
- Lens choice - brings the background forward

- Vertical and landscape orientation
- Shooting towards space

Step 2: Position the subject in the frame

- Visual anchor - the point of fixation
- Emphasis and dominance of focal points
- Hierarchy of focal points and visual flow
- The rule of thirds
- Left to right
- Framing
- Positive and negative space
- Active space
- Repetition and pattern
- Isolation
- Mergers
- Juxtaposition - colors, tones, texture, height, shape

Step 3: Position the supporting elements

- Figure to ground
- Proximity - unity and abundance
- Common fate - similarity
- Scale
- Lines - horizontal, vertical
- Lines - different types of diagonal
- Implied line of sight
- Converging lines - vanishing and diminishing point
- Triangles
- The Fibonacci spiral golden spiral
- Rhythm, time and motion
- Color contrast - triadic and split complementary

- Gesture and interaction

Step 4: Enhance composition using mobile editing tools

- Border Patrol
- Vignetting
- Removing items
- Shadows and crushing the blacks
- Lens flares
- Removing distracting objects

The FULL List of Composition Techniques and Tools

Step One - Set Up and Position the Camera

Camera height - subject
Camera height - background
Camera height - foreground
Subject to lens distortion
Lens compression
Perspective – lens distortion
Tilt distortion
Symmetry - vertical, horizontal
Symmetry - spiral and radial
Symmetry - crystallographic
Asymmetrical balance
Unique perspective - look up
Unique perspective - ground level
Light - direction and quality
Light - hard light
Light - Side lighting

Flat lay - bird's-eye view
Reflections
Over-the-shoulder
Keystone distortion
Two-point perspective
Three-point perspective
Diminishing perspective
Atmospheric perspective
Forced perspective
Orientation and aspect ratio
Corner to corner
Shoot toward space
Vertical panoramic
Walking panoramic
Dutch angle

Step Two - Position the Subject in the Frame

How does the eye work?

Visual anchor

Emphasis - dominance

Off-centre

Rule of thirds

One-third - two-thirds

Left to right

Centred

Frame within a frame

Negative space

Positive space

Active space

Repetition and pattern

Isolation

Avoid mergers

Fill the frame

Proportion

Silhouette

Juxtaposition - colours/tones

Juxtaposition - time/objects

Eye contact

Step Three - Position the Contextual Elements

Closure	Golden spiral
Figure to ground	Fibonacci spiral
Proximity	Baroque diagonal
Common fate	Focal points - hierarchy
Continuance	Foreground interest
Similarity	Framing
Minimalism	Rule of odds
Scale	Layering - distance
Lines - leading	Layering - overlap
Lines - diagonal	Rhythm, time and motion
Lines - s-curve and z-curves	Colour - monochromatic
Lines - horizontal	Colour - harmonious
Lines - vertical	Colour - contrast
Line - implied line of sight	Colour contrast - advanced
Lines - converging lines	Subject research
Triangles	Gesture
Golden ratio	Interaction
Phi grid	The decisive moment of action

Step Four - Enhance Composition - Mobile Photo Editing Tools

Visual tension	
Straighten	Local adjustments
Cropping	Selective tool
Perspective	Masking
Expand tool	Masking
Selective sharpness	Selective colour
Linear sharpness	Vignette
Gradation	Light flares
Shadows/highlights	Removing distraction
Shadows - Crush the blacks	Reposition elements

About Mike James

After twenty-five years of working in the technical field of photography, I disliked taking photos in my own time. It was in 2015 when my mum passed away, that I then realised how many precious memories were never captured. We only have six photos of my mum in her last nine years with our three children.

So, suspending my extreme prejudice toward the smartphone, I took regular photos. I didn't need to worry about the camera setup. I could slow down and capture the beauty of the world around me. I fell in love with mobile photography!

I wanted to share my passion and help amateur photographers. So, I ran local mobile photography workshops and became a prolific content creator. The discovered fulfilment of training led to study and qualification in training design and assessment.

I may not travel to exotic places to create content or have a huge social media following. But, I can help you become the mobile photographer you want to be in a short time. This book is a brilliant first step!

Learn more at **www.smartphonephotographytraining.com**

Reviews

A very comprehensive look at composition

"Mike James has put so much thought into this book. If you've ever wanted to know anything about composition, one of the most important fundamentals of photography, look no further. I've been practicing photography for decades and Mike's book has introduced me to a lot of new ideas regarding composition. Mike James is brilliant and this book is a must-have for any photography enthusiast. A superb learning tool."

- Greg McMillan - The iPhoneography Podcast

Content-rich - exceeds any other book or YouTube

"I never thought someone could provide so much detail on photo composition. I truly do not believe there is another book that covers composition to the depth that is taken in this book. The detail goes well beyond framing a subject and using grid lines to make sure you place your subject properly. I have taken classes and read books that cover photo composition but no one has ever spent this much time to cover the topic to make sure you get it right."

- Tod W

An exceptional addition to the world of photographic thought and technique

"Mike offers his readers, in a most accessible way, an outstanding approach to composition, as he combines all of his learning from the last 20 years of photography to help everyone else take amazing photos. His warm manner of reading and engaging personal style makes his book very easy and enjoyable to read. Being a photographer myself, I am excited to let you know that I have personally gained so much from his wisdom and experience. I know you too will benefit."

- Ralph Mayhew Photography

The go-to book for photo composition.

"This an absolute must-buy for anyone interested in photography who would like some help with composing better photos. I cannot recommend this book highly enough, it is superb, in clear, precise language, and with some great photos for illustration. Don't hesitate just buy it, you won't regret it. Thanks, Mike for this wonderful aid in improving my photos."

- Mark Johnson

Over-the-top comprehensive

"The book is jam-packed with everything you will ever need to know about photo composition. There are photos to show you what works best and the written content tells you why it works. It will become my "go-to" reference book for composition"

- James Della Volpe